MANAGEMENT IN THE NETHERLANDS

MANAGEMENT IN THE NETHERLANDS

PETER LAWRENCE

CLARENDON PRESS · OXFORD

1991

Oxford University Press, Walton Street, Oxford OX2 6DP

Oxford New York Toronto
Delhi Bombay Calcutta Madras Karachi
Petaling Jaya Singapore Hong Kong Tokyo
Nairobi Dar es Salaam Cape Town
Melbourne Auckland

and associated companies in
Berlin Ibadan

Oxford is a trade mark of Oxford University Press

Published in the United States
by Oxford University Press, New York

British Library Cataloguing in Publication Data
data available

Library of Congress Cataloging-in-Publication Data
Lawrence, Peter A.
Management in the Netherlands/Peter Lawrence.
Includes bibliographical references (p.   ) and Index.
1. Industrial management—Netherlands.   2. Industrial
organization—Netherlands.   I. Title.
HD70.N4L39   1991   658'.009492—dc20   91–13023
ISBN 0–19–828684–8

Typeset by Butler & Tanner Ltd, Frome and London
Printed in Great Britain

To
Katy and Patrick

Acknowledgements

I WOULD like to thank Technische Hogeschool Twente, as it then was (now Universiteit Twente), for offering me a research fellowship in 1985, and for the help and friendship shown to me there by former colleagues in the Afdeling der Bedrijfskunde (Management Department). I would also like to thank Geoffrey Gregory, my former head of department at Loughborough University, England, who was kind enough to contribute to the expenses of my research work at this time from departmental funds. This sojourn at Twente was my first opportunity to get to know something about Dutch industry and Dutch management at first hand.

Four particular people whom I got to know at Twente in this period have been helpful throughout my research, with ideas and comments, introductions and favours, materials and reading, and above all good stories. They are Jan Kreiken, former Head of the Management Department and now Professor Emeritus of Universiteit Twente; Jan van Dalen, now Professor at the Openbare Universiteit (Open University) at Heerlen; Hans Heerkens, now Lecturer in Management at Universiteit Twente; and Jacques van den Meer, now Professor of Corporate Strategy at Groupe ESC Lyon.

What I like to think I have come to know and understand about Dutch management has been learned 'on location' in Dutch commercial and industrial organizations, rather than 'slaving over a hot databank' in the library. So my most critical debt is to the managers and staff at the more than fifty companies I visited in the Netherlands in the 1985–90 period, who gave up their time to talk to me about their work and offer me their views. Their contribution was indispensable.

At the same time I do not wish to hide behind the testimonies of the people I talked to. I asked the questions and decided what were the most interesting bits of the answers; the patterning and interpretation are all mine, and so are the errors.

Finally, I would like to thank Nanette Vickers, my secretary in the spring of 1990, for a priority word processing of the manuscript.

P.L.

University of Loughborough
May 1990

Contents

1

Reaching Parts Others do not Reach

THE Heineken slogan that its beer reaches parts other beers do not was meant as a pun on a medical analogy. But it also makes good sense geographically.

Soon after the ending of Prohibition in the USA, and barely a month after Roosevelt was sworn in as president for the first time, the following note appeared in a leading American newspaper: 'The first legal shipment of imported beer in thirteen years arrived in Hoboken, NJ; it was about 100 gallons from the Heineken brewery in Rotterdam, and was brought here on the SS Statendam as a test shipment' (New York Times, 14 April 1933). It was the start of an enduring relationship, and an expanding market. In 1988 a total of 47 million hectolitres of beer was brewed by or under the supervision of Heineken. Of this total some 10.3 million hectolitres were sold in the Western hemisphere and a substantial part of this in the USA. Today Heineken is the number one imported beer in the USA.

America represented a particularly attractive market, but not an isolated successs. Even a quick glance at Heineken's annual reports reveals an impressive coverage around the world. In France in 1988, for example, Heineken increased its interest in Sogebra SA from 52 to 100 per cent—its operating company produces Heineken. In Spain Heineken has a majority interest in El Aguila SA; in Italy it has Birra Dreher SpA. In Greece Heineken has the Athenian Brewery SA, and again 1988 was a good year. In Ireland the lager segment of the market expanded in the same year, and Heineken is the market leader. Although sales of stout are declining in Ireland, Heineken's operating company, Murphy Brewery Ireland Ltd, actually increased its sales of Murphy's Irish Stout.

Great Britain, where Heineken is marketed and brewed under

licence by Whitbread, showed a modest increase in 1988. Similar under-licence arrangements are in place in Norway and Sweden, while Portugal and Switzerland are served by direct export. Mind you, it is not, as they say, all beer and skittles in European beer sales. The Netherlands' closest neighbours, Belgium and West Germany, are not only countries where beer is drunk with conviction, they are also leading beer producers. In short, they are not easy markets, and in the case of Germany the challenge is accentuated by the fact that there are so many breweries, mostly regional or local. There is, so to speak, no German Whitbread, that could be a national distributor. But then again neither Europe nor America is the whole field. Heineken has a foothold in Canada with Amstel Brewery Canada Ltd (Amstel is part of Heineken), representation all round the Caribbean, and a presence in South America. In Africa Heineken has a brewery in the Congo where Amstel is marketed under the slogan: *Plaisir raffiné—plaisir partagé* ('a refined pleasure, a shared pleasure'). Heineken has a bottle factory in Zaire, as well as interests in breweries in Zaire, Rwanda, Barundi, Réunion, Morocco, Angola, Cameroon, Nigeria, Sierra Leone, Ghana, and Chad.

It goes without saying that Heineken has a licensing agreement in Japan, and an expanding export market in Australia; it has also held on to its market share in Jordan and Lebanon. At the end of 1988 it was announced that Heineken had taken a minority stake in a brewery in Shanghai.

Lessons

Internationalism is a cardinal feature of business life in the Netherlands. Heineken is not a unique example, though it is a good one. To put this example in perspective, it is worth asking whether Bass or Whitbread or Grand Met has a stake in breweries in Shanghai and Chad, and a big slice of the US foreign beer market—and if not, why not.

Heineken may be a giant, but it is not from a giant country. In geographical terms, the Netherlands is smaller than most US states.

With a population of 15.5 million at the start of the 1990s, it has not much more than a quarter of the population of Britain. Yet it has been able to spawn some big companies. The presence of these big multinational companies in such a small country is another distinctive feature of Dutch business life. Again, Heineken is a good example of this phenomenon. Heineken is the largest brewery in the Netherlands, though by no means the only one. Taking Western Europe as a whole, there are four breweries that might be described as European in terms of their cross-border sales and operations. These are Kronenbourg of France, Carlsberg of Denmark, Stella Artois (Interbrew) of Belgium, and, of course, Heineken. Actually, Heineken is the biggest of the four. Indeed it is number three in the world league, after the American giants Anheuser Busch (Budweiser) and Miller Brewing. In fact Heineken is the most successful exported beer in the world. It has exported more beer than any other single country—no matter how many national brands are combined.

Ways and Means

There is more. Heineken is not just big, it is adaptable—and that is another strength of Dutch business. Heineken sometimes establishes its own breweries in other countries, and sometimes it buys, in whole or in part, breweries in other countries. Sometimes it simply manufactures (or distributes) under licence, as with Whitbread in the UK. And sometimes it serves a foreign market by importation—from Switzerland to the USA. It is worth pausing to consider the last option: imagine serving the vast American market by shipping the goods across the Atlantic—and doing it for sixty years.

But it is the adaptability in the choice of market access that should be emphasized. It represents a conscious and thoughtful response to life's exigencies. As one Heineken manager I was talking to put it:

So why don't we call them Heineken Spain or Heineken Italy or Heineken whatever it may be? The main reason is, as we see it, they are operating on their local market, producing local brands and corporate brands, and they are to a large degree independent from headquarters, and we want to stress that they are independent local companies, of course having ties with Heineken, but we want to stress that they are local and independent by their name.

This does not go without saying. There are, for instance, few American companies that would play it this way. This ability to play down nationality, to assimilate and adapt, is very Dutch. Nor is Heineken a unique example. Philips is another past-master.

Outside the Netherlands Philips is adept at low-profile representation. You do not see Philips of the Netherlands abroad, but, say, Philips of Malaysia. Or, to take a European example, for decades Philips traded in Britain under the name of Mullard. Half the British population probably did not know that Mullard was Philips (and the other half thought Philips was Welsh rather than Dutch anyway).

This lack of nationalism in business is not manipulative. The Dutch simply do not feel a need to assert national identity through their corporations. Being accepted, being able to adapt, being able to do business—from Toronto to Timbuktu—is enough for them.

People Besides Operations

There is another dimension. Internationalism is not just about contributions to profit, passages in the annual report. It is also about people, and many of these people are Dutch. There is contemporary interest in the idea of the 'European manager', the cross-border executive who can do it outside the homeland. There is interest in this breed, but not seeemingly very many of them. Yet some gneralizations do seem possible. Small countries are better at producing European managers than big countries. Language proficiency, whether natural or acquired, is critical. And the ability to go abroad, but without parading your national origins, is perhaps decisive. It is not entirely clear how the Dutch do it—after all they do not lack a sense of national identity and a pride in their homeland—but clearly they do achieve it. And it shows at the level of postings and placements. As a small example consider the international character of the appointments at Heineken reported in the company's December 1988 *International Magazine* (reproduced below).

APPOINTMENTS

Mr. P. Hamers, factory manager at the Heineken brewery in 's-Hertogenbosch, has been appointed regional technical manager Africa. He succeeds **Mr. G. Slootweg,** who has been appointed general manager of the Yimin Brewery in Shanghai (China) with effect from 1st January next. The new factory manager in 's-Hertogenbosch is **Mr. A. de Voogd,** until recently technical manager of New Zealand Brewery Ltd.

Mr. P. Lebru, formerly marketing director of Bralima in Zaïre, has been appointed general manager of Brarudi in Burundi. He takes over from **Mr. A. Verwilghen** who has transferred to the post of financial director at Ibecor, Brussels. **Mr. P. Hottois** has taken over Mr. Lebru's marketing responsibilities. **Th. M. Zwart** is the new technical director of Bralima in Zaïre in succession to Mr. Levèbvre.

Brasserie de Brazzaville is to have a new general manager. The post will be filled by **Mr. J. L. Homé,** whose previous job was that of deputy financial director at Française de Brasserie.

The new marketing manager at El Aguila in Spain is **Mr. L. Alcácer.** He has succeeded **Mr. F. Bot** who has been appointed project manager within Coordination Europe.

Newly appointed as factory manager of the Heineken brewery in Zoeterwoude is **Mr. H. de Goederen.** He succeeds Mr. H. Kloek who, as previously announced, has been appointed director of beer production for the Netherlands. Mr. De Goederen's former posts were as brewery manager in Ghana, Sierra Leone and Lagos (Nigeria).

Another Beer, Another Thought

Heineken has served as an ideal example to introduce the themes of internationalism and adapatability in Dutch business life. And at a more homely level Heineken is certainly a company thought of in Britain as having cut a dash with witty and memorable adverts. But Heineken is not the only company to show virtuosity in this field.

The second largest brewery in the Netherlands is Grolsch. It is not on the scale of Heineken, but it is a middle-weight rather than a local brewery. It is very strong in the eastern parts of the country, but sells all over the Netherlands; in an interview in the late 1980s one of its directors referred to exporting 17 per cent of product (Piet, 1987). Grolsch has its headquarters and main site in the eastern city of Enschede, and another brewery in the small town of Groenlo to the south of Enschede—there is a joke in the Enschede area that this is the most egalitarian part of the Netherlands because everyone can drink Grolsch.

It is indeed a nice beer, with an old-fashioned quality aura—the beer your father drank, as it were. It is also retailed in distinctive swing-top bottles from the Groenlo brewery. In the early 1980s Grolsch was marketed under the slogan *Vakmanschap is meesterschap* (something like 'Expertise is mastery') which catches exactly the notion of old-fashioned quality. Then later in the decade it seemed, judging from the adverts, that a wider customer base was being courted. New adverts showed Grolsch being drunk by young people, girls, Indonesians, and even Rastafarians; in cafés, at the roadside, in the billiard saloon. The next generation of adverts showed a similar range of people, with the accompanying exhortation: 'One day, stop drinking beer and just drink Grolsch'. It became a set phrase in the Netherlands. The apotheosis, at the end of the decade, was an advert showing a cooled, inviting, just opened bottle with the heading: 'One day . . .' Simple, but evocative.

Story or Parable?

There is an English tendency to think that the English have a monopoly on the whimsical and engaging, including things like clever adverts. They do not: the Dutch can do it as well. But there is another issue. It is often said of the Dutch that they have all sorts of virtues, but are inhibited and unimaginative. This is not a silly judgement. There are all sorts of indicators of conformism and anti-individualism in Dutch society, some of which does impinge on management and will be explored in a later chapter. But at this point it might be helpful to offer a more qualified judgement. The Dutch are inhibited by this tendency to conformity; it may on occasion mask imagination, originality, and *élan*, but these qualities are there. They are also in evidence in Dutch business life, and not confined to engaging advertising.

2

An Institutional Mosaic

T H E vignette of the outgoing Dutch offered in the previous chapter gives rise to a further question. What are these Dutch like, who sally forth so resourcefully and adaptively, and in particular what is their 'home base' like? It is generally accepted that those whose adventurousness takes them abroad are empowered by the twin forces of national assertiveness and domestic unity. From the Jomsborg Vikings of the eighth century to the British colonial administrators of the nineteenth, vigour and shared values have underlaid conquest and colonial adventure. To give a more obviously commercial example, the Japanese of the latter twentieth century, who have succeeded abroad on an epic scale with their exports and more recently with their foreign manufactures, are notable both for their sense of national purpose and for the homogeneity of the domestic springboard. But what of the Dutch?

In this, as in so much else, the Dutch do not conform. Heterogeneity at home, with cultural and institutional differences, has been the backdrop to their business internationalism. And these are considerations of which the Dutch themselves are conscious, indeed proud. While, as noted in Chapter 1, the Netherlands is actually smaller than most US states, the Dutch expounding on their regional variation make it sound at least the size of Canada. The good Dutchman is at least instinctively aware of the institutional density of the country, knows no foreigner will ever understand it, and sometimes even mildly resents the attempts of outsiders to learn the language (better off listening to insider accounts in English). This heterogeneity has several dimensions.

Verzuiling

The Netherlands, with its restricted land mass and population of around 15 million, exhibits some remarkable and distinctive features. These include the level and intensity of regional differences, the permanent coalitional nature of national politics, and a parade of public affluence that is equalled only in Scandinavia. But perhaps the most distinctive is the (one-time) importance of formal religious allegiance and a patterning of both institutions and aspects of social life in terms thereof. The Dutch call this *verzuiling*, or pillarization, a term which has become semi-familiar in English through the comparative politics and political sociology literature. In the strict and strong sense *verzuiling* is a thing of the past, but of the relatively recent past. The formal patterning of many institutions along confessional lines still exists, and there are some intangible residues as well.

It all began in the sixteenth century, in what in British history books is known as the Revolt of the Netherlands—against Spanish overlordship; in Dutch history this is known as the Eighty Years' War (1568–1648), with the independence of the seven provinces constituting what we know as the Netherlands being formally and finally recognized by the Treaty of Westphalia in 1648. In the revolt and protracted war of independence, three provinces were dominant, the traditionally Calvinist western seaboard provinces of Noord Holland, Zuid Holland, and Zeeland. These three were economically dominant and made economic gains from the ousting of the Spanish; they were the powerhouse of the revolt, militarily and politically, and they (especially Zeeland) produced the so-called *watergeuzen* or water pirates, radical Calvinist pirates who preyed on Spanish shipping. All this gave special status to Calvinism: it is associated in the Dutch context with liberation and glory, prosperity and resolution. Other areas of the present-day Netherlands had a less pristine record in those heroic times. Some towns like Groningen in the 'deep North' only went over to the goal of Dutch independence relatively late; others like Deventer in the east changed hands and sides several times.

Wars in the sixteenth and seventeenth centuries were not

fought continuously but in campaigns. This ragged intermittency was further accentuated by the problems of financing the armies, whether mercenary or patriot. In practice, therefore, there was a continuing cycle of conquest, withdrawal, and reconquest as armies ran out of money, disbanded, and reformed with new funds. In short, the Eighty Years' War was a complicated mosaic of thrust and counter-thrust. The dominant role of the western Calvinist provinces is one of the few consistent elements. This hegemony was continued in the later seventeenth century by the pre-eminence of the same areas in what is known as the Golden Age—a renaissance of art and literature, underpinned by commercial success. The Golden Age did not occur in up-state Overijssel, but in the west, and especially in the cities of the west.

The religious map of the Netherlands in the modern history period has the south Catholic, with the west, north, and east Protestant. More precisely, the two southern provinces of Brabant and Limburg are Catholic, with only small Protestant minorities; the adjoining province of Zeeland is 'northern' in religious and cultural terms, even though situated in the south-west. The rest of the country is Protestant, though with much larger Catholic minorities, for example in the east. The Catholics have in the past experienced some civil disabilities, and even today the monarch must be Protestant.

By the nineteenth century, religion, region, and even historic reputation were loosely overlapping and reinforcing each other. Institutional segregation was given a further thrust later in the century by the two dominant issues: extension of the franchise (beyond middle-class males) and (confessional) control of the growing educational system. Liberal elements wanted both extension of the franchise and state-controlled schools, while the religious parties wanted confessional schools. Over time a complicated trade-off emerged, with large-scale enfranchisement on the one hand, and a curious tripartite system of schools on the other—state schools, Catholic schools, and Protestant schools, with all three options at least theoretically available at both primary and secondary level. Furthermore, the growing organizational apparatus of an industrial society was also structured confessionally, with

Protestant and Catholic political parties, trade union blocs, and employers' organizations. In the mid-twentieth century the main institutional change was a coalescence of Catholic and Protestant organizations, so that in the three areas just mentioned there are now religious and lay political parties, trade union blocs, and employers' organizations.

Several things should be added to this account. First, *verzuiling* was not just a matter of formal organizational distinctions, but something that was lived and felt. Not just trade unions and political parties, but everyday things like bookshops, sports clubs, and recreational organizations were *verzuild*, or segregated confessionally. In mixed population areas, Catholics would go to the Catholic baker's shop and Protestants to the Protestant baker's, *and* such practices would be exhorted from the pulpit.

Second, *verzuiling* was and is seen as connoting something in human character terms. Now there is more to regional differences in the Netherlands than a simple north versus south contrast, yet this contrast is basic, in the sense that the character of the Catholic provinces of Brabant and Limburg is presumed to be in contrast to the rest.[1] People from these areas are thought to be more optimistic, charming, life-loving, unreliable, and wedded to 'the outer features'—the candles in church, the garments the priest wears, and so on. They are more deferential, status-conscious, gracious, and inclined to be bon vivants; they celebrate Christmas more colourfully, but avoid quarrelling intransigence when it comes to their ideology or preferences (unlike the Calvinists who love a bit of stoical intransigence). Some of this is carried over to the Catholic schools as well. Indeed Catholic primary schools are sometimes preferred by non-Catholic parents on the grounds that they are more relaxed and child-centred than Protestant or state ones.

Third, there is a certain sense in which *verzuiling* has been a boon for social integration, in the sense that these religious-based differences are cross-class ones: they run counter to class divisions and do not reinforce them. Thus the Netherlands is one of the many countries in the industrialized world that can claim a relative absence of social class distinctions. In so far as this claim is justified, *verzuiling* has been a contributory factor.

Fourth, *verzuiling* is not simply a phenomenon of the distant past; it certainly persisted into the 1950s, and even in the 1990s you can point to a number of at least formal organizational cleavages on confessional, or religious versus lay lines, including:

- Political parties: one of the major parties, the CDA (Christelijk Democratisch Appel), is a 'general purpose' Christian party, formed by the fusion of three separate Catholic and Calvinist parties as late as 1977 (cf. West Germany, where Catholic and Protestant interests were merged in the CDU party by 1949). There are also three small extreme religious parties which do not form (coalitional) governments, but do have parliamentary representation, and may also come to power in a few *gemeenten* or local authority areas and enact there religious based policy options.
- Schools, as already mentioned. Tilburg and Nijmegen are also Catholic universities, while Amsterdam has a Protestant university.
- The media, with radio and TV time shared out on an ideological and confessional basis.
- Trade unions, organized into parallel blocs, one primarily socialist (the result of an earlier merger between Catholic and socialist unions) and one Christian.
- Employers' organizations, with a non-religious, liberal–conservative federation, and a Christian, primarily Calvinist one.
- Hospitals: at least it is usual to have a Catholic one and a state and/or Protestant one, and the Catholic hospital is likely to have different policies on the sensitive matters of abortion and euthanasia.

There are also several very strict, and rather closed, Calvinist communities flourishing in the 1990s, including the townships of Urk, Harderwijk, and Staphorst. Perhaps the best known of these is Staphorst, Overijssel, which makes a most appealing visual impact. Many of the inhabitants, of all ages, wear a traditional costume of which the dominant colour is royal blue. This blue recurs in the colouring of the dwellings, many of which have the same deep-blue gates, doors, window boxes, and window sills. The houses themselves are 'ideal type' Dutch houses with their intimations of cosiness and orderliness. Yet this same community achieved a certain notoriety in the 1970s: forswearing polio vaccination on religious grounds, it later suffered a polio outbreak.

It is well known that Dutch Catholicism has developed in liberal and modernist directions; indeed, Dutch Catholics achieved some notoriety in the mid-1980s for their rather hostile reception of the Pope.[2] Again, though I have written simply of Calvinism, there are in fact two main strands. First, there is the *hervormde* church, which Dutch people describe as 'more modern'. Then there is the *gereformeerde* or strict Calvinist church, which dominates, for instance, the fishing community of Urk on the coast of the Noordoost Polder.[3] In addition there are some minority strands, such as the Article 31 Community, a strict sect formed, improbably, in 1944.

All of the foregoing may create the expectation that the Dutch are a spectacularly religious nation, and that this will show up in church attendance. After the 1977 general election a survey was made, showing the following self-reported rates of weekly church attendance for the three groups: 40 per cent for the Catholics, 25 per cent for the *hervormde* Calvinists, and 77 per cent for the *gereformeerden*. These rates seem high, though perhaps less than we might expect in view of the socio-religious history of the Netherlands. Yet perhaps more interesting is the reaction of many Dutch people when presented with these figures; almost 'to a man' they reject them, scoff at them, dismiss them as vast overestimations deriving from an amalgam of unreliable self-reporting and foreign gullibility. This impasse suggests another question: is *verzuiling* still important in some way that goes beyond the formal practice of religion?

In response it might be argued that there are at least connections between the dominant Calvinist tradition and certain national character traits that many of the Dutch themselves claim, and those mentioned here all have some implications for the character of management. First, there is the ethic of incorruptibility. It may be that Dutch businessmen are not any more incorruptible than British ones, but they tend to think they are, and think that it is something worth talking about. On several occasions, when Dutchmen in a position to make international comparisons were asked to say what they thought was distinctive about Dutch management, lack of corruption was high on their list. There was also a tendency to contrast the Netherlands in this respect not only with some Third World nations but also with other countries in Western Europe. This must be a Calvinist legacy.

So, too, is the steadfast element in the Dutch character. If you know what is right, you must stick to your guns, and one can sometimes see Dutch people taking an almost morose satisfaction in doing so. The 'something' that you stick to may be a matter of principle, as in the case of corruption, or in the management context a mattter of organizational procedure, or of factual or circumstantial detail. The Dutch do observably like their details and will not be gainsaid on them.

An undoubted Dutch virtue, and one they like to talk about, is reliability. They take commitments seriously, and are scrupulous in their execution. As with corruption, this is a feature sometimes mentioned by Dutch managers, but it comes up more often in what might be termed the 'battle of the regions'. When asked what is the 'real difference' between the north (with its Calvinist tradition) and the south, people typically answer in terms of contrasted reliability. The reply goes like this: 'When someone from [name your favourite northern province] says he'll do something, he'll do it. But when a southerner promises to do something, well...'[4]

There is also the Dutch understanding of individuality, which must owe something to Calvinism. The individual is a unit of moral accountability, not a Renaissance star. There are norms and endless proverbs condemning eccentricity, boastful pride, and self-glorification. Life is not, in the words of the Fame song, 'a celebration' but a trial, and conformity is a Dutchman's best friend. This emphasis on not being different, not setting yourself apart, not playing tunes of glory, is fairly easily uncovered in discussions with Dutch managers, and it colours attitudes to such subjects as promotion, ambition, corporate posture, and leadership.

Finally, in this connection, there is the fact that religion, or at least its socio-cultural heritage, overlaps with region and serves to reinforce the Dutchman's understanding of regional difference. This sense of region in turn acts against the geographical mobility of employees and is thus a brake on manager mobility.

Regionalism

Dutch people speak about regional differences frequently and with evident relish. In the Dutch mind there are lots of regional differences and they are important. First, there is the basic north–south difference, roughly corresponding to the Calvinist–Catholic difference explored in the previous section. As one person put it: 'Really we think there are two basic kinds of Dutchmen: those who live above, and those who live below the rivers.' The rivers in question are the Rijn/Lek (Rhine), the Waal, and the Maas (Meuse), rivers that roughly speaking flow from right to left across Holland. Indeed the phrases *boven de rivieren* and *beneden de rivieren* ('above the rivers' and 'below the rivers') are standard expressions in Dutch. So is the more picturesque *Boven de moerdijk*, the *moerdijk* being a famous bridge over the Hollands Diep on the road north from Breda to Dordrecht.

This north–south divide is presumed to connote temperamental and behavioural differences. It is a case of happy Catholics versus reliable Calvinists, or their socio-cultural heirs.[5] One person from Rotterdam (in the Netherlands you really have to know where people are 'coming from') apostrophized the south in this way: 'Limburg and Brabant, there they like status, honour, glitter, good food, and good wine. They are more creative, less work obsessed, more stylish and more artistic. They have more charm and are less blunt.'

Cutting across the north–south divide is the east–west divide, where the west is the *Randstad* area dominated by the four major towns—Amsterdam, Rotterdam. The Hague, and Utrecht. This gives us the city versus country dimension. Depending on your reference point, people from 'the West' are modern, articulate, sophisticated, and born to rule, or a bunch of decadent, self-important, bumbling radicals.

Furthermore, although the towns of the west are mostly within half an hour's drive of each other, they are seen by the Dutch as differing in ambience as well as formal character. The Hague is the diplomatic, administrative, and political capital; Amsterdam is the commercial and cultural capital (as well as the real capital); Rotterdam is the big industrial town with the world's largest harbour. The Rotterdam–Amsterdam comparison is particularly intriguing: Rotterdam is very much Birmingham or Lyon rather than London or Paris, the straightfoward, no-nonsense place were work gets done. There is indeed a joke in Dutch that Rotterdam is where you make money, Amsterdam where you spend it, and The Hague where you talk about it.

Do the regional differences matter, or are they simply a sociological curiosity? It can be argued that they have some background—and at points even intrinsic—importance in a discussion on Dutch management. First, 'the regions' provide a kind of economic geography of the Netherlands. The northern provinces of Friesland, Groningen, and Drenthe, for example, are relatively poor and largely agricultural, while the heavily populated area in the west that the Dutch call the *Randstad* is highly urbanized, highly industrialized, and relatively rich.

Indeed, the American concept of the section, where a section is a georgraphical area with a distinctive economic interest, could also be applied to the Netherlands. The *Rijnmond* (the Rhine above Rotterdam estuary with harbour and petroleum refinery interests) is one such; Twente in its heyday as the textile centre of Holland was another; so is the Westland area between Rotterdam and The Hague, as the centre of gravity of the Dutch market garden industry, and so on.

Second, the provinces may engage in economic planning and *gemeenten* (townships, local government areas) in economic initiatives. The mayor and council of the city of Enschede in the eastern province of Overijssel, for example, have not only engaged in the kind of initiatives that have been common in various countries in the 1980s—co-operation with the technical university in the region, making available business premises, and so on—but have also developed more sophisticated strategies for economic development and job creation.

One such strategy aims to develop the Enschede area as a distribution centre, taking account of its nodal position in between the *Randstad,* and the towns of the west, especially Rotterdam, and the Ruhr in West Germany; indeed many goods entering the Netherlands in the west pass through the Enschede area en route for Germany and Scandinavia; this, together with the plentiful supply of cheap premises in Enschede, is a powerful reason for locating distributional facilities in the Enschede area of Overijssel. Another key strategy is the provision by the Overijssel Ontwikkeling Matschappij (development organization for Overijssel province) of venture capital for business start-ups. It concentrates particularly on high-tech. enterprises with a minimum size threshold, and specializes in attracting Scandinavian and American companies to establish operations in the Overijssel area.

Third, the regional differences probably yield corresponding differences in the workforce climate in factories. Certainly personnel officers whom I interviewed referred to differences in the workforce by region in terms of deference, radicalism, company loyalty, work-centredness, and propensity to stay or leave. Fourth, again coupled with religious differences, regional differences are probably a brake on mobility, certainly on mobility of labour, and, albeit to a lesser degree, on the mobility of managerial talent. Finally the suspicion exists that regionalism has some effect on managerial appointments. This is usually denied by the Dutch, typically arguing from the model of the multinationals. The multinational companies, of course, recruit nationally, and deploy and rotate executives nationally: they are, no doubt, above and beyond regionalism. But it may well be the (unmeasurable) case that regionalism constrains applications to non-multinational companies, and I strongly suspect that small firms, especially family firms, tend to appoint managers who are co-regionalists and/or co-religionists. Certainly entertaining stories to this effect are not difficult to come by.[6]

Politics

It would be fair to say that the structure of politics in the Netherlands differs in several ways from that of Britain or the USA. In short:

- There are more parties, big and medium-sized, with parliamentary representation.
- A number of these parties are religiously based.
- Coalition governments are normal.

The three biggest political parties are:

1. The VVD (Volkspartij voor Vrijheit en Demokratie—People's Party for Freedom and Democracy). The rise of the VVD is relatively recent (1980s), and is usually depicted as the concomitant of *ontzuiling*, or of the decline of *verzuiling*.
2. The CDA (Christlich Demokratische Appel, or Christian Democrats), on the other hand, represents the consolidation of the religious vote; it derives from an amalgamation of three separate Catholic and Calvinist parties in 1977.
3. PvdA (Partij van de Arbeid, or Labour Party) is (at the time of writing) actually the largest single party in terms of seats in the lower house, and regained power in a coalition with the CDA after the election in the autumn of 1989.

It should be added that not only are there a lot of parties in the Netherlands, but they share a relatively small number of parliamentary seats. The upper house has 100 seats, the members being chosen by province, while the lower house, or Tweede Kamer, the equivalent of the British House of Commons, has 150. This means that all the parties' numbers are small. So, for example, the VVD had around ten seats in the mid-1970s; by the mid-1980s, when the party was in power in a coalition with the CDA, they were thought to have done remarkably well with 25–30.

Then there are the smaller parties. Between the VVD and the PvdA on the political spectrum is Demokratie 66, the digits referring to the year of foundation, not the number of deputies. On the left there are several parties smaller than the PvdA, including the CPN or Dutch Communist Party, the PSP or Party for Socialist Pacificism, the EVBP—a very small party based on progressive Christian principles, the PPR—a radical party with its roots in one of the parties presently in the CDA, and the Schoten Partij—a one-deputy party owing its existence to the secession of its leader from the CDA because of personal antipathy to apartheid. To the right of the VVD are another four parties, the SGP, the GPV, and the RPF, all Calvinist-based parties, and the Centrum Partij, a party with fascist leanings and no religious basis, which did well at the time of its first entry to parliament but which later split internally. This is the Dutch *embarras du choix*. It is interesting not only as regards the presence of the various exclusive confessional parties as well as the omnibus CDA, but also as regards the breadth of the spectrum finding organized expression.

Coalition is the normal form of government. The present (1991) administration is a CDA–PvdA coalition, and the most likely, but not immediate, alternative would be a coalition of the ubiquitous CDA with another party or parties. Again, it should be added that a general election is not always *immediately* followed by the institution of a government (governing coalition). The talks which precede the birth of a working coalition are typically complicated and sometimes protracted.

It is no more than a personal interpretation, but I suspect that this parliamentary government model—differentiation, negotiation, compromise, and coalition—represents a peculiarly Dutch way of doing things. Or, to put it another way, the Netherlands lands is not a 'winner takes all' society, unlike, say, the USA, but a bargaining–wrangling forum which proceeds by adjustment.

Finally, it is interesting to see that the loose regional–religious overlap noted in the earlier discussion is again discernible in the electoral support of the various parties. So, for instance, the largely Roman Catholic south is the natural constituency of the CDA, while the PvdA has not traditionally been strong there. The west, and especially its larger cities, has the lowest rates of church attendance, so voting here is more on class lines, that is, split between the VVD and the PvdA. The north and the east, however, vote according to religion, choosing between the various Calvinist parties and the CDA, with the non-religious vote again going to the PvdA or the VVD, with the communists having a stronghold in Groningen.

Mayors are also chosen along party lines, so that if the majority of the elected council in a *gemeente* is, say, PvdA, then a PvdA mayor is likely to be appointed. The appointment is formally made by the queen, but *de facto* by the government of the day. In most cases, however, there is little room for manoeuvre; only in the case of a 'hung council' can the government exercise any discretion in its own favour. And the 'mayoral geography' follows loosely the model presented in the last paragraph. In the West, Amsterdam and Rotterdam have PvdA mayors, but Wassenaar (a wealthy residential area north of The Hague) and Utrecht are VVD. Maastricht (Limburg province, deep south) has a CDA mayor, as does The Hague itself. The Twente area in the east offers a new twist to the mayoral story: Enschede, the large manufacturing town, has had a PvdA mayor since 1945, whereas in the two neighbouring towns of Hengelo and Almelo the CDA rules: in Hengelo the CDA mayor is a Catholic, and in Almelo a Protestant.

In so far as there is a 'party of business' it is undoubtedly the VVD, one of the coalition partners until the autumn 1989 election. Yet the identification of the VVD with business is not overpowering; it is not like the Republican Party in the USA. Indeed, the administration of which the VVD was part until 1989 saw as its primary goal the reduction of public expenditure, a much more dynamic issue in the Netherlands than in Britain. Both the government and current attitudes are entirely favourable to business, entrepreneurialism, free enterprise, and wealth creation. Yet the former CDA–VVD administration will probably be best remembered for its virtuosity in holding down wages and salaries, and effecting at least indirect wage reductions.

Education

The education system, like the political, is marked by a high level
of differentiation: not only are schools differentiated by religious
or state affiliation (see under *Verzuiling*, above), but also at the
secondary stage by pupil ability level. In this the Dutch system is
more like the West German than the comprehensivized British
system. There is also a certain symmetry about the Dutch system,
where the various types of secondary school feed different types
of higher and further education establishments, as is clear from
Figure 1, adapted from an official publication (Ministry of Education
and Science, 1979).

Nursery school[7] is universally available, free, and compulsory
in the Netherlands and covers ages 4–6.[8] The child then attends
primary school from 6 to 12. In the autumn of 1985 the two types
of school were officially amalgamated nationwide and given the
name of *basisschool*.

The primary schools, as noted earlier, are of three types—
Catholic, Calvinist, and state—though the choice made by parents
may well not be a religious one. To give a positive example: as
noted earlier, the Catholic schools tend to be regarded as more
relaxed and are sometimes chosen by non-Catholic parents on
these grounds. To give a negative example: the state primary
schools tend to attract the children of non-Christian foreign workers
and are sometimes avoided by ambitious, middle-class (agnostic)
parents for this reason.

At the age of 12, at the end of primary school, there is a test,
recommended but not compulsory, on the basis of which allocations
are made to the various types of secondary school. In fact parents
may ignore this '12 plus' recommendation, and send their child
where they like, as long as he or she can keep up. In all the Dutch
secondary school types the pupil must pass the end-of-year exams
(in part based on a continuous assessment system) in order to move
on to the next year. If a pupil fails, they repeat the year, and if
they fail *the same year* twice, the consequence is transfer to another
type of secondary school (moving to the right in Figure 1). It
would seem that sizeable numbers do repeat years and there may

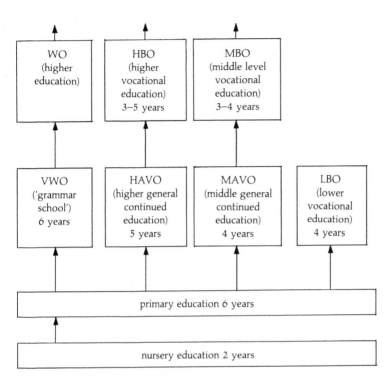

FIG. 1. The Dutch education system

also be cumulative repetition (e.g. a pupil does the first year twice, then the second year twice, and so on), with the effect that any given class may contain a minority of significantly older pupils.

The Secondary System

In the secondary system, the VWO (*Voorbereidend Wetenschappelijk Onderwijs*, or preparatory academic–scientific education) is an institutionalized university stream, taking only a minority of the age group. VWO education lasts from ages 12 to 18. VWO establishments are further divided into the Atheneum (common) and Gymnasium (relatively uncommon); in the Gymnasium Latin and Greek are offered as extra subjects and Gymnasium attendance is said to confer a little additional prestige. There appears to be subject specialization in the last two years of VWO, where pupils follow the A stream or B stream. The A stream is arts–humanities: Dutch, maths, plus two other languages, plus other arts subjects to a total of seven. The B stream consists of science subjects plus Dutch and one other language, again totalling seven. All subjects from each of the two streams are taken in the final exam, known as the *Eindexam*, so the Dutch VWO student has in English terms the equivalent of a seven-subject 'A' level.

Homework (*huiswerk*) is a serious issue in the Dutch secondary-education system, and reaches its apogee in the VWO schools. There the idea is that in the first year the pupils have one hour's homework per night, in the second year two hours, and so on up to a stupendous six hours a night in the sixth year (though Dutch students I have asked differed on how far this was enforced in practice). This theoretical sixth year homework burden is modified in practice by the fact that Dutch and the other language subjects include a lot of set books, and reading these is counted in the six hours (for two languages this would be something like 40 books over a two to three year period).

The *Eindexam*, the Dutch equivalent of 'A' levels, is taken in late April or May. Pupils are allowed to fail two subjects without having to repeat the year, these being retaken at the resit exam in July. The results are graded on a scale going up to ten, where five is a fail and six a pass, and it is unusual to get more than eight. These grades, however, are for performance in individual subjects, English style; there is no overall grade like the *Abiturdurchschnittsnote* in West Germany. If you pass the *Eindexam* you have the right to go to university, and, in theory at least, study anything anywhere. In practice, this freedom is limited by the need to have laid the specialists basis at VWO level for later university study, and a few university courses are subject to a *numerus clausus* (actually the expression in the Netherlands is *numerus fixus*). The standard example of a *numerus fixus* subject is of course medicine, and the new star in the *numerus fixus* league is management. The fact remains that passing the *Eindexam* does confer the right to enter university, not just to be an applicant, as is the case in Britain.

The next secondary school type, HAVO (*Hoger Algemeen Voortgezet Onderwijs*, or higher general continued education), is a scaled-down version of VWO. The course lasts one year less, the end-of-course specialization is in six rather than seven subjects, and 'graduation' from HAVO does not admit to university but to the HBO or higher vocational education system. MAVO (*Middelbaar Algemeen Voortgezet Onderwijs*, or middle general continued education) is scaled down again, a four-year course ending at the age of 16 (at least for those who do not repeat years). MAVO 'feeds' the MBO or middle-level vocational education system. Both HAVO and MAVO have a curriculum and *modus operandi* of a formal academic kind; they have regular progress exams, exam-based year-to-year promotion, lots of homework, and a good range of academic subjects. To take foreign languages as an example, both HAVO and MAVO pupils do English and French in the first year and add German in the second.

The last secondary type, LBO (*Lager Beroeps Onderwijs*, or lower vocational education), differs from the other types in being, usually, an end in itself: it leads directly to work (and apprenticeship) rather than to another tier of the vocational education system. Furthermore, although the general title of LBO is used here, there are all sorts of variations on the theme: LTS schools offer junior technical education, HSS schools a domestic science education, LEAO schools a preparation for junior administrative and clerical jobs, and so on. In the late 1980s at any rate there was a certain amount of folk wisdom in favour of the LBO as a secondary school choice. The argument runs, in effect, 'If you don't think you're an academic high-flier, for goodness sake do something practical that

links up with a real job.' Certainly there are voluntary transfers
from MAVO to LBO.

Before outlining the higher and further vocational education
systems, it is only fair to say that in the Dutch secondary system
the formality is tempered by flexibility. The system is exam-
oriented, but with institutionalized arrangements for resits and
repeats. Transfers between the types are institutionalized as well,
and not just in the sense of moves 'downwards' for under-achieve-
ment. Pupils can, for example, move from MAVO to HAVO by
completing the fourth year at MAVO, then moving sideways to
HAVO and repeating the fourth year there. Similarly, pupils can
move from HAVO to VWO by completing the HAVO fifth year
and repeating it at the Atheneum. Some VWO 'graduates' also
elect to move on to the HBO or higher vocational education
system rather than exercise their right to go to university (depicted
as WO in Figure 1).

The Universities

Dutch universities are very much on the Continental rather than
the British model. As already mentioned, all who pass the *Eindexam*
are free to enter; they also have longer courses, larger taught
numbers, and higher dropout rates. Although there is no university–polytechnic distinction as in Britain, the university–technical university distinction is formal and explicit, on the West
German rather than the British model.[9]

There are twelve universities in the Netherlands: the Erasmus
University in Rotterdam, two universities in Amsterdam (one
Protestant and one non-Protestant), Catholic universities in
Nijmegen and Tilburg, both in the south. There are also universities
in Leiden, Utrecht, Groningen, and Maastricht, in Limburg
province, the latter being the most recently established university.
Then there are, or were, three technical universities: Delft,
Eindhoven, and Twente. Delft is the old, established one in the
west. Eindhoven was set up after the war, in 1948; it is strong on
electrical engineering and electronics (Eindhoven is the Philips
home town and world headquarters). Twente in the east was

established in the 1960s as a technical university but converted to being a 'general purpose' university in the later 1980s.

The Dutch make a lot of there being no Oxbridge or Ivy League in the Netherlands; only individual departments or professor groups achieve a standing above the average. This is undoubtedly true in a formal sense: there is no university which has a special entry system after the manner of Oxford and Cambridge, and the universities and the degrees they award are nationally accepted as being equal in a formal sense. The Dutch claim is also true in a relative sense: whatever informal differences one may point to among the universities in the Netherlands, they are not as large or as widely accepted as those in the UK or the USA.

Having said that, there are some differences of prestige and aura, though I do not want to make too much of this. These differences can be explained in three ways, with differences often overlapping. First, there is the old Dutch precept that the West outranks the Rest; other things being equal, the universities on the western side of the country do enjoy an extra element of prestige. Second, age confers dignity; Amsterdam, Utrecht, and particularly Leiden, and among the technical universities Delft, gain in this way. Third, there is sometimes a difference of political coloration or perceived aura, so that Amsterdam and even more Groningen are seen as somewhat to the left, and Rotterdam and even more Leiden are seen as to the right. Leiden, indeed, seems to enjoy a little bit of Ivy League lustre, and the Leiden law school (and occasionally the Utrecht law school) is quite often mentioned as something of an old boys network. On the subject of connections, the Netherlands' 'management university' at Nijenrode should be mentioned. Nijenrode originally offered management training but was not a degree-giving institution; it now has university status and awards degrees, but is exclusively concerned with management education. It is said of Nijenrode that it is concerned with developing social and presentational skills, and cultivating contacts; it is also keen on sport. Certainly you meet many well-placed managers who trained there.

What Degrees do Managers Have?

If you proceed from an account of the higher education system to the question 'What do managers in the Netherlands study?', a fairly clear-cut answer is possible. By and large, Dutch managers who have been to university have studied engineering, economics, or law, and in some cases an engineering course has been 'topped off' with some management teaching.

This predominance of engineering, economics, and law, with engineering in first place, is what some writers see as the continental system in contradistinction to the British. Ian Glover, for instance, has seen similarities along these lines in the pattern of management qualifications for a number of continental European countries (Glover, 1978), including West Germany (Lawrence, 1980) and Sweden (Lawrence, 1982).

There is also a throughput of graduates in management, though, with the exception of Nijenrode, this is a relatively recent phenomenon (1980s). Apart from Nijenrode, management degrees may be done at the universities of Rotterdam and Groningen, and at the technical or former technical universities of Eindhoven and Twente. Among all the graduate managers I met in the Netherlands in the 1985–90 period, the only ones who had studied management had done so at Nijenrode and Twente, but undergraduate management courses are booming nationally and management graduates are bound to 'show up' more clearly in the executive subject mix of the future.

The Higher Vocational Education System

The HBO (higher vocational education) system is extensive in the Netherlands and somewhere between 10 and 15 per cent of the age group passes through it. HBO is a general name for the range of vocational educational colleges, fed primarily by the HAVO schools at secondary school level but with diagonal or transfer input from VWO and MAVO (see Figure 1).

The level of training offered by the HBO system is something like that of the (old) Higher National Certificate/Higher National

Diploma standard in Britain; the HBO colleges in turn are some-thing like Britain's area technical colleges or West Germany's *Fachochschulen*.

HBO is an umbrella term, so groups of colleges within the system specializing in different subject or occupational areas are known by different names or initials. Thus, for example, there are some thirty-four HTS colleges, specializing in various branches of engineering;[10] teacher training colleges; SA (*Sociale Akademie*) colleges training social workers, and more recently people for personnel jobs in the private sector; HEAO colleges doing econ-omics and commercial subjects; a number of HEAO colleges pre-paring people for non-engineering jobs in industry; a police training academy, and a *Bestuurs Akademie* training civil servants for the provincial administrations. The HBO system is flexible. It provides both full-time and part-time courses. The part-time offering is growing, especially in technical education, and is not age-restricted. People on the full-time courses will generally be in the 17–25 age range.

Direct entry to the HBO system is via the HABO (or VWO) leaving certificate; for the typical entrant this means a six-subject exam taken at the age of 17 that is, somewhat more than 'O' levels in England. There is a growing number of people passing the *Eindexam* at VWO, and thus qualified for university entry, who are in fact opting for HBO. This is explained in general terms as a vote in favour of the vocational and specific, as opposed to the academic and general, but also in some cases in terms of fear of the univer-sities' unstructured learning ethos—the HBO system is more organized and disciplined, more like a continuation of secondary school. To this one may add the practical consideration that there are many more HBOs than universities and so more choice geographically, and more chance to live cheaply at home. In this connection, if we take engineering as an example, there are now only two technical universities, but thirty-four HTS (i.e. engineering HBO) colleges. One particular consideration for those opting for HBO rather than university is that HBO developed computer science courses at an earlier stage than the universities and these are thought to offer particularly good employment prospects.

Lecturers in HBO colleges will be either HBO graduates them selves or, more probably, university graduates. There are a few areas described as 'free', where the lectures may not be required to have formal qualifications, for instance in fine arts teaching, and there may be exceptions to the university graduate principle where a corresponding university course does not, or has not, existed.

HBO lecturers typically have practical experience as well as formal qualifications and this experience is likely to be measured in years—though it should be noted that this practical experience is not a national legal requirement, as it is in, for instance, West Germany (Hutton and Lawrence, 1981). The practical experience requirement in the Netherlands is most likely to be waived these days when the HBO system cannot match the private sector (commerce and industry) salaries of specialists in, say, economics, some branches of engineering, and computer science. Interestingly, it was the other way round in the 1960s and 1970s, with salary levels being higher in education. HBO students themselves engage in practical training as part of their course. The practical placement usually lasts around six months and typically occurs in the third year of the HBO course.

Finally, the HBO system underwent a change in the late 1980s. Amalgamations of HBO colleges, typically colleges in the same area but with different subject specialisms, have been strongly encouraged. This amalgamation policy is inspired by the desire to cut costs, but there is also by a conviction that larger HBO colleges will be better able to develop contacts with the occupational world and to compete with the universities. The new HBO law that came into effect in 1986 put the financing of the HBO system on a par with that of the universities, and encouraged the HBO colleges to engage in research.

There are two reasons for spending some time looking at the higher reaches of the Dutch education system—university and HBO. First, managers in the Netherlands who hold formal qualifications—and most do—are qualified at these two levels. Furthermore, the HBO system is very versatile and is providing training and a qualificational base for a variety of functional specialisms in commerce and industry. Second, the system is on the whole rather well geared to the needs of the economy. While it is possible to make criticisms—the HEAOs (HBO colleges for administration) were developed too recently; the SA (*Social Akademie*) colleges concentrated exclusively on social work training for too long; the 'system output' of people with computer training is too small; too few people enrolled on engineering courses in the 1970s, causing a corresponding shortage in the 1980s; there is too much pressure on undergraduate places in management, and so on—the system as a whole, together with its capacity to adapt, must be counted a national strength.

Companies

There are two basic kinds of company with limited liability in the Netherlands, the NV (*Naamloze Venootschap*) which has quoted shares, and the BV (*Besloten Venootschap*) with non-quoted shares. It would appear that the non-quoted type (BV) have a higher relative importance in the Netherlands than in Britain. But perhaps more striking is the fact that Dutch companies do not have a single board of directors but two types of board.

Dutch public companies in fact have a two-tier board system, as do public companies in, for instance, West Germany. At the top is the *raad van commissarissen* or supervisory board, consisting entirely of non-executive directors. Non-executive directors are those who do not work full-time for the company concerned; their contribution is primarily in the form of attending board meetings and in preparation for them. The *raad van commissarissen* is appointed by the *Andeelhoudersvergadering*, or shareholders' meeting. Below this is the *raad van bestuur* or executive board, consisting exclusively of executive directors, that is, those who are full-time senior managers in the company concerned. The *raad van bestuur* is appointed by the *raad van commissarissen*.

The Raad van Commissarissen

In normal times the *raad van commissarissen* will not be especially active and the company will actually be run by the *raad van bestuur*. The *raad van commissarissen* is, however, likely to intervene in a crisis, such as a crisis of confidence in the personnel of the *raad van bestuur*, or in decisions relating to capitalization and the global nature of company operations. The normally quiescent role of the *raad van commissarissen* can perhaps be indicated by the annual report of one such supervisory board of a major company.

Paragraph 1 of the report presents the annual accounts, announces the profit, designates a certain sum as retained earnings, and proposes a dividend of *f* 7 per ordinary share. But perhaps the next paragraph best indicates the even tone of proceedings:

We met seven times in 1984. Much of our time was devoted to matters requiring regular attention, such as the annual report and dividend proposal, half yearly figures, budgeting, the report on social matters and strategic planning. Moreover, a number of times the Executive Board asked our approval for intended acquisitions. In all our meetings the Executive Board reported on the course of business and informed us of the items dealt with in the consultative meetings with the Central Works Council.

The following paragraph promises more excitement, in that one meeting considered a proposal to close a loss-making division, but it did not happen, an outside buyer was found who continued to run it. The last four paragraphs refer to personnel changes in the *raad van commissarissen* (whose turn to stand down next year, and suchlike concerns) and to the timing of meetings. And that is it, the activities for the year of a supervisory board of a household name company doing unquestionably well.

What kind of people become members of these supervisory boards? There are several answers. First, the *raad van commissarissen* is to some degree a prestige barometer for the company concerned: an illustrious company must have illustrious *commissarissen*, as the supervisory board members are called in Dutch. This is particularly true in the case of the leading multinational companies. Second, and related to this, there is often an international flavour to the supervisory board, with members who are not necessarily Dutch nationals but drawn from countries where the company has a major customer or operating presence. Third, some companies use supervisory board membership as a reward and 'final corporate resting place' for former managing directors and senior executives. Fourth, there is a certain amount of overlap among the latter, with the same sort of people turning up on the supervisory boards of different companies. You do not need to spend long in the Netherlands to be able to recognize recurring names in the annual reports of Dutch public companies. Here are the observations of one senior executive on the subject of supervisory board membership:

You judge a company by the prestige of its *raad van commissarissen*. You ask, are the members people who have been presidents or had senior posts in other companies. In ABN (one of the leading banks), for example, you will find high-powered people from Shell and Unilever. Of course, banks are a special case; they like *raad van commissarissen* members from customer companies ... Sometimes companies take ex-prime ministers, even people from foreign governments. It has got very international in the last ten years. My company? We have several non-Dutch members, the head of a German bank, another one recruited as a specialist in East–West trade. Our supervisory board meetings are in English, it is the same at Shell, Unilever, and Philips. Also some of the multinationals appoint senior executives to the supervisory board when they retire; Philips does this, they like to have old Philips hands who know that business. Hereditary nobility? Yes, we have one. In fact, unlike England, it is only hereditary. The person is *Jonkheer*. Philips and some big companies have them on the supervisory board, but only if they are good.

On the subject of the role and function of the supervisory board, this same executive commented: 'You can have a good company with a bad *raad van commissarissen*, so long as it has a good management. But not the other way round.'

The Raad van Bestuur

Not so the *raad van bestuur* or executive board: this is the body which really runs the company and it has to be good. This is not a truism. There are countries where this board is a formalized showpiece and real executive decisions are made elsewhere; the *styrelse* of public companies in Sweden is a case in point (Lawrence, 1982).

Use of the term *raad van bestuur* to denote the executive board is relatively recent, a development of the last twenty years or so. Previously the executive board was known as *de direktie*, an expression that is still used conversationally. Though one speaks of a chairman (*voorsitter*) of the *raad van commissarissen*, the corresponding term for the chairman of the *raad van bestuur* is *president-direkteur*—the Dutch equivalent of managing director or chief executive officer (CEO). As noted earlier, the *raad van bestuur* is appointed by the *raad van commissarissen*; in theory (law) they do not have the right to designate the *president-direkteur* as such, but in practice it does happen.

A study of the larger companies in the Netherlands, reported to the author in 1985, showed that 60 per cent of *raad van bestuur* members were university graduates. Of this 60 per cent over half were engineering graduates—though the numerical dominace of engineers is held to be diminishing—and the rest were largely graduates in law and economics. Since that time the twin trends are towards higher formal educational qualifications, and in favour of economics and management as qualification subjects.

It may be helpful to take a few examples from some of the best-known companies in the Netherlands. At Philips the *raad van bestuur* is made up mainly of engineers with a few accountants. At Unilever the *president-direkteur* is in fact a non-graduate. At Shell both the present CEO and his predecessor are economics graduates. KLM is run by a lawyer (from the Leiden law school), and his predecessor was an ex-air force general. AKZO (a chemicals multi-national) is run by a chemical engineer, as is DSM (Dutch State Mines, literally, but actually another chemicals company). Hoogovens (steel, heavy engineering) is run by a mechanical engineer, the two leading insurance companies by a lawyer and a statistician respectively.

It is also worth raising the question of the structure of the *raad van bestuur*. The functional executive board, on which directors represent specific functions such as sales and production, is the normal type for smaller companies in the Netherlands, the functions most likely to be represented being finance, production, marketing, probably R and D (research and development), and personnel. Alternatively companies may have a divisional executive board, divisions usually being based on product (range) or process, rather than market territory. So, for instance, a steel company may have heavy steel, light steel, and tubes divisions. But probably the most common type overall is the mixed executive board that combines functional and divisional appointments.

Finally, in this connection, it is worth raising the question of the relative prestige of the various functions—sales, finance, R and D, and so on. In the heyday of searching for reasons for British economic under-performance, a lot of play was made with this notion of differential functional prestige. One argument spawned in this debate was that finance is an overvalued function in British companies, leading to restraint, retrenchment, and risk aversion. Another was that production, design, and engineering were undervalued, leading to a lack of emphasis on technical innovation, quality, and reliability. The question is: does any of this find a sympathetic echo in the Netherlands?

The standard Dutch answer is no, there are no generally or readily acknowledged differences in the standing of the various management functions. Given similar responses in West Germany and Sweden, the proposition can probably be accepted at face value, though it is fair to add some qualifications.

First, interviewees provided some interesting speculations on the prestige of the personnel function, traditionally low to medium but arguably on the way up. Second, what is happening to the production function in the sense of current perceptions and priorities may be changing as the economic environment changes, variously emphasizing design virtuosity, quality, the streamlining of production, and cost efficiency. Third, some people actually cited production and/or the technical functions as the key areas. Philips, with its high R and D spending, is a case in point. As one executive put it: 'If it were purely a matter of research brilliance we would have beaten the Japanese hands down.' The Venlo-based copier company Océ, again with an above industry average spend-

ing on R and D is another example of a company that puts design
top in prestige terms. The Dutch are, however, as suggested earlier,
very attached to their egalitarian norms, so there may well be an
element of wishful thinking in their denials of status differences—
especially when given to an enquiring foreigner. The issue will be
raised again in a later chapter, and looked at in the light of salary
differentials.

In this chapter we began by raising the question as to whether the
Dutch drive abroad is fuelled by a single-minded homogeneity at
home. It is clear that it is not, that the Netherlands is in fact marked
by heterogeneity as to historical experience, region, and religion.
What is more, this diversity is manifest in the 'organizational
geography' of the Netherlands—a theme we have explored with
respect to politics, the education system, and the structure of
companies, working out at various points the implications for
management.

   A further generalization is in order. Not only is the 'organizational geography' a rich field of study in the Netherlands, in the
sense that there are lots of bodies and structures and organizational
parallelisms, but it has another quality. The Netherlands is marked
not only by organizational complexity but also by articulation and
conditionality. Organizations and systems connect with each other,
balance each other, depend on or constrain each other. This latter
idea will be give a further thrust in the next chapter where the
focus will be on employer and more particularly employee organizations, and the bargains made between them.

Notes

   [1] I was once asked in the east if I had ever been to the Netherlands before,
and I mentioned holiday visits to Heerlen and Maastricht in Limburg. This evoked
the response 'That's not Holland, it's Italy'.
   [2] Once I visited a big church in a major town in the Catholic south. There
seemed to be no holy water, I could not identify any confessionals, and there
was such a wealth of anti-papal propaganda on display I was convinced this was
a Calvinist house of worship; Dutch friends later identified it as a famous Catholic

church. There are not many countries in which this kind of mistake is possible.

³ In the late 1980s the two Calvinist churches announced their intention of uniting (Shetter, 1987).

⁴ I have heard this one repeatedly, almost in the same words, from a variety of people.

⁵ I have actually come across the phrase 'happy Catholics' several times from Dutchmen exploring this basic dichotomy of the Dutch character.

⁶ Just to give the flavour of this genre, I was told of a Catholic company in a Protestant area that went to some trouble to appoint a good Catholic to the board of directors; the appointee was also homosexual and later formed a highly visible liaison with the local mayor.

⁷ In the Netherlands the nursery schools are not referred to as kindergarten; the Dutch name is *kleuterschool*.

⁸ The compulsory nature of school attendance is taken very seriously in the Netherlands. It is difficult to keep children off school for any reason other than illness, and there is some reluctance to fudge the issue, as is common in Britain (fudging is not a Dutch speciality).

⁹ Though several universities in Britain did have the word 'technology' in their title at one time, all have shed it except for Loughborough University of Technology, University of Manchester Institute of Science and Technology, and University of Wales Institute of Science and Technology.

¹⁰ As of 1979 (Ministry of Education and Science, 1979).

3

The Two Sides at Work

W H I L E Class consciousness in the Netherlands is much less marked than in Britain, and much less important as a guide to style and behaviour, as in so many other areas in the Netherlands, the interaction between the 'two sides of industry' has given rise to a more elaborate organizational apparatus. As the sympathetic American observer William Shetter put it: 'The Dutch have a noticeable preference for imposing a visible, familiar structure on any kind of social structure, down to the most casual. In the Netherlands, in other words, association of any type is a natural extension of the value the culture places on careful organisation' (Shetter, 1987: 117).

In the present context the interaction is structured via trade unions, employers' organizations, and the machinery of industrial democracy. Organizational complexity is also buttressed by documentary refinement in the form of the numerous collective work agreements (CAOs) negotiated each year between the trade unions and the employers or employers' organizations.

Employers' Federations

As in West Germany, employers' organizations in the Netherlands have a more important place in national economic life than is the case in Britain. They are among the organizations in the Netherlands that are *verzuild*, or organized along confessional lines, as discussed in Chapter 2, though these confessional lines have been modified by amalgamation so that there are now two federations, one lay and one religious.

The VNO (Verbond van Nederlandse Ondernemingen, or Federation of Dutch Enterprises), the non-religious federation, is the larger of the two, and the one most expressly keen on free enterprise values. The smaller, religious-based employers' federation is the NCW (Nederlands Christelijk Werkgeversverbond, or Dutch Christian Employers' Association). These two employers' federations interact with the corresponding trade union organizations, especially in the matter of pay bargaining.

Trade Union Organizations

There are two corresponding trade union confederations, again showing the same impact of *verzuiling* and amalgamation. First is the FNV (Federatie Nederlandse Vakbeweging, or Federation of Dutch Trade Unions), the larger and probably the more radical of the two, which derives from an earlier merger of socialist and Catholic unions. The CNV (Christelijk National Vakverbond or Christian National Trade Union Federation) is the smaller one; in the research interviews it was often described both as 'primarily Protestant' and as 'an arm of the CDA', the CDA being the major Christian political party, described in Chapter 2, and one of the present (1991) coalition partners. But this is not the whole picture. In addition to these two *quasi-verzuilde* trade union confederations there is a third one, for higher grade employees. This is known as Unie BLHP (Beamten Leidinggevend en Hogere Personeel).

In looking at the structures that exist below these three confederations, it is helpful to discard certain British categories at the outset. In short, the British distinction between craft unions, general unions, and industrial unions does not fit the Dutch system. Nor does the German model of industrial unions only where the number of unions is very small (seventeen plus misfits), and typically all employees in a given industry, for instance the chemical industry, join the same union (if they want union membership). The German model is mentioned here because it is often thought of as a polar opposite of the British in its clear-cut simplicity. The Dutch system is not like either of them.

The three union confederations are made up of constituent unions. Let us take the FNV, the largest, as an example. Some 19–20 unions make up the FNV, and these include:

- police
- military
- government employees (now the largest union, as in Sweden)
- transport workers
- building workers
- service sector employees
- food industry employees (a legacy of large-scale agricultural employment)
- typographical union
- an industrial trade union, which includes workers from manufacturing industry (with some exceptions); this used to be the largest single union.

This system of constituent union membership is reproduced on a small scale in the CNV, and in a modified way in Unie BLHP. None of these unions would satisfy the German criteria for industrial unions, both because of blue-collar replication as between the FNV and CNV and because of white-collar creaming off by Unie BLHP. Most of the constituent unions do satisfy the looser English understanding of industrial unions, with the same qualification about CNV and FNV replication, but some are general unions in English terms, most obviously the large industrial workers union; and in practice the Dutch typographical union mentioned above is probably equivalent to an English craft union.

Union Funds

Depending on whom you ask, Dutch trade unions are 'jolly well off' or 'under considerable financial pressure'. If you say that there are some 1.2 million members who pay around *f*200 per head per year, that there are government subsidies, that companies make per capita payments to the confederations in appreciation of the latter's role in developing the collective work agreements (CAOs), and that the unions have savings and pension fund income, it sounds as though they are 'sitting pretty'. The other side of the story is this.

The 'organization rate', or proportion of people who choose to join trade unions out of the larger number eligible to join them, was about 35 per cent in the late 1980s, though traditionally in the Netherlands it is somewhat higher at around 40 per cent. Membership went down because of:

- the recession of the early 1980s
- rationalization/automation
- government policy in the sense of unpalatable decisions the unions could not do much about, for example, expenditure cuts and wage rise capping in the 1980s
- the fact that women and younger workers are coming to constitute a higher proportion of the labour force but are traditionally less 'unionizable'
- companies using the opportunity of the 1980s recession to decentralize pay negotiations, which meant a loss of standing for the large confederations.

Other difficulties of the trade unions

In addition to the drop in membership—and therefore income—experienced by the Dutch trade unions in the 1980s, two other difficulties should be mentioned. First, the public–private sector split both accentuates CNV and FNV differences and cuts across them. The CNV is more public sector-oriented, with some 60–70 per cent of their membership drawn from the public sector, including civil servants, police, military, and teachers. The FNV, on the other hand, is about 40 per cent public sector and 60 per cent private. What is more, public sector organization rates are tending to rise, while private sector ones are declining. At the same time, the private sector–public sector divide cuts across the CNV and FNV difference, so that private sector CNV unions probably have more in common with FNV private sector unions than with public sector unions affiliated to their own CNV. Second, the Dutch trade unions are in a situation in which nationally the total workforce has declined significantly over the last ten years or so, and older workers who have lost jobs have tended not to get new ones. In practice this means that the negotiating posture of the unions is vitiated by the gulf between members who actually have jobs and want wage rises (especially if they are young married couples with children) and unemployed members who want policy change concessions. The latter group are also more likely to have time to attend union meetings!

Trade Unions and the 'Labour Party'

The relationship that we take for granted in Britain between the trade union movement and the Labour Party is not replicated in the Netherlands. The Dutch trade unions do not contribute funds to the Partij van de Arbeid described in Chapter 2, nor are there trade unions MPs in the Netherlands. There are, however, contacts between the trade union confederations and employer's organizations on the one hand and the major political parties on the other. Of course, in a pluralist country like the Netherlands everyone talks to everyone else. Three inter-organizational dialogues are, however, more than averagely cordial, namely those between

- the CNV union federation and the CDA (Christian party)
- the FNV union federation and the Partij van de Arbeid
- employers' organizations and the VVD or liberal party.

Pay Bargaining

The traditional model, from after the Second World War until about 1980, is that the CNV and FNV and Unie BLHP bring their claims to an intermediate organization, the Stichting van de Arbeid, in The Hague. The employers' organizations then respond, and negotiations take place between these and the trade union confederations, resulting in a number of CAOs (*Collective Arbeids Overeenkomst*, or collective work agreements). As a (large-scale) footnote to the traditional model, it should be added that the very big companies have always dealt directly with the unions rather than via the employers' organizations. With these exceptions, however, a high level of centralization has prevailed, with the government in the role of 'watchdog'.

With the onset of the depression in 1980, a trend towards decentralization occurred, with all substantial firms tending to act independently. As a result deals are now more likely to be between branches of industry and unions, groups of firms and unions, or even single firms of lesser size than previously and unions. When single firms or groups of firms negotiate they will typically be supported by adviser-representatives of the employers' organizations, the VNO and NCW. These are held to be particularly good at drawing union fire and taking the pressure off company negotiators. The end product is again the CAO.

The companies clearly prefer this 1980s decentralization. It gives them more direct control, more chance to get settlements relevant to particular operating circumstances, and more chance to exploit individual corporate strengths. But the trade union confederations, of course, are fighting it. They can argue that in a relatively small country such as the Netherlands, a centralized system is much more viable than it would be in, say, Britain. The government, of whatever coalitional colour, also has some interest in the centralized system, which facilitates a measure of control and intervention. In the cost-cutting climate of the 1980s and early 1990s, for example, the government has an interest in getting both sides to trade off *arbeidstijdverkorting* (shortening of the working week) against wage rises.

Wage Negotiation: A Part Example

One of the companies I visited in the 1980s described the last round of wage bargaining that had resulted in a CAO. This was very much a 'spirit of the times' example in that the company concerned, a family firm with some 800 employees, 'went it alone', conducting its own negotiations with the three union confederations. On the company side, the negotiations were carried out by the chairman, assisted by the company personnel manager and advisers from the employers' federations.

Perhaps the most interesting part of the whole process was its inception. It all started with the three union confederations writing to the company concerned and setting out their demands. The points raised offer an interesting sidelight on the character of union objectives: .

1. The duration of the CAO agreement to be negotiated was itself an issue, with companies in favour of longer-lasting agreements and the unions wanting (to revert to) shorter ones.
2. The reallocation of labour was an issue, in the sense of providing more jobs through *arbeidtijdsverkorting* (shortening of working time).
   (a) A 32-hour working week was proposed for 1990 (the company concerned had a 38-hour week as of 1985, and expected to move to 36 hours in 1986).
   (b) Retirement: 65 is the national retirement age. This company has a system of retirement at 62 for long-serving employees; the union proposal was to reduce this to 60.
   (c) Holidays: the proposal was to increase from 24 to 25 days.
   (d) Overtime: the proposal was to reduce it to zero.
3. An increase in the *vakantietoeslag* (an extra month's salary paid as a holiday bonus in May) was proposed.
4. The proposed wage rise was:
   1.5 per cent at start of contract (CAO), year one
   1 per cent in mid-year, year one
   1.5 per cent at start of year two
   2 per cent in middle of year two
   i.e. 6 per cent over two years.
5. The Dutch government had reduced sick pay and introduced a ruling obliging workers to pay national insurance contributions while sick. The trade unions asked for this to be made up by the company (under the previous CAO the company already guaranteed employees full pay for two years in the event of sickness).
6. The trade union letters pointed out that in the late 1990s the increase in the labour force would stop, stabilize, and then decline, and asked if the company had taken this on board and was developing appropriate policies.

7. A similar point was raised about youth employment. The two issues are related in that youths might be unemployed from the mid-1980s until the second half of the 1990s and then be needed, never having worked before.
8. The company was asked to find more practical training places for MBO students, that is, students from vocational training colleges.
9. The unions asked for equal treatment for men and women employees in respect of promotion and training.
10. Finally, the unions demanded control of and involvement in technical developments, which hitherto had been the concern of management and staff. In this matter unions were asking for a say in when, whether, and under what conditions technical development would be allowed to take place.

Now the company concerned did not grant all these demands. It 'boxed clever' on some, side-stepping them or neutralizing them by claiming they were already covered by other agreements. But the content and style of the demands is most interesting. First, there is the extreme modesty of the wage demand, even in a mildly recessionary period. A cynical Briton might ask, if they were prepared to settle for 4 per cent why they did not ask for 10 per cent to give themselves room for manoeuvre. By British standards Dutch workers demand and get a good deal from their employers, but they are not troublesome in the central matter of strikes or threatening to strike. The Netherlands has had a low level of strikes throughout the period since the Second World War, including the 1970s which seem to have been more euphoric in the Netherlands than anywhere else. In the above set of demands, the wage demand does not dominate and does not even seem particularly central.

Second, the reverse side of the demand picture is interesting. There is, that is to say, a high level of past gains and future expectations on hours, holidays, extras, sickness benefit, and retirement rights. This is very Dutch: the CAO negotiation used here as an example is quite typical. Such gains are peripheral in British terms. The right to time off reaches on occasions horrendous proportions. It is quite common for the worker's right to a day off for his mother-in-law's silver wedding anniversary to be written into the CAO: no Dagenham shop steward in his wildest moments would think of this!

Third, the whole demand set is redolent with Dutch values—concern for others, equality, serious-mindedness, and the long-term view. The issues raised reflect concern for women, youth, the sick, and the aged. Only the Dutch could ask a family firm in the mid-1980s what policies the company had for dealing with fluctuations in the birth rate which would affect the structure of the labour force in and after 1996—*and keep a straight face.*

The Pattern of Collective Work Agreements

Although these collective work agreements (CAOs) are by definition industry or company specific it is possible to generalize about them. First, although there are something like 700 CAOs drafted and negotiated each year, they are all the result of an orderly, predictable, and well-understood process of initiation and negotiation, exemplified in the previous section. The various parties do not suddenly initiate a CAO negotiation because they have just thought of something they want or feel like a change. There is a proper time for these things, and a due process that is widely accepted.

Second, the CAO is a middle-term instrument for regulating relations between employees and companies. A CAO is not a 'quick fix' or a patch-up job, but neither does it commit the parties for periods of years at a time. Traditionally the CAO was for one year, but as has been noted the trend in the 1980s was for companies or employers to press for a longer period of validity. At the end of the 1980s and beginning of the 1990s there was some variation in this matter. The CAO for the Limburg glass industry in 1988, for example, was for a duration of one year, while the CAO of the same year for newspaper journalists was for eighteen months. Also in 1988 Grolsch (the brewery whose imaginative advertising was discussed in Chapter 1) and Unilever both negotiated CAOs of two years' duration, as did the printing industry in 1989.

Third, if we look at a series of CAOs between particular bargaining parties they are of course marked by continuity and incrementalism. Especially on the employee side there is an attempt to build on the achievements of the past, to push concessions in particular areas a little bit further, as is clear from the example offered in the last section. Nor is this policy of serialized incrementalism to be found only on the trade union side any more. Employers have come to push increasingly for CAOs of longer duration. This gives employers more stability, aids corporate planning, and not least frees senior management from the need to engage in demanding and often protracted negotiations at annual intervals.

Fourth, although pay demands tend to be modest by British standards, the details of the wage agreement fill a considerable part of the CAO as a written document. Seemingly endless pay scales are listed, crossed with age, grade, and seniority factors. As a result the CAO booklet, typically reproduced in the form of a reduced typescript, serves as a useful source of reference and comparison for employers (Geddes 1990).

It was remarked jocularly in the discussion of the Dutch education system in Chapter 2 that 'fudging' is not a Dutch strength. This is not to say that the Dutch are inflexible; on the contrary they are willing to listen, bargain, and consider a variety of viewpoints. But they are not inclined to 'fudge' in the sense of saying one thing and doing another, or of using a deliberately vague formula to permit a variety of (questionable) practices: these, of course, are British proclivities. The Dutch dislike of fudging finds natural expression in the CAO, which is not only contractual in format but spells out everything that can be spelled out, making it clear, quantifying it, not leaving anything to chance or, still worse, to discretion.

A particular example of this phenomenon is the matter of time off. The one day off to celebrate your mother-in-law's silver wedding anniversary is just the tip of the iceberg. Entitlement to time off for such contingencies as births, deaths, and weddings is conscientiously inscribed in the CAO. These entitlements are naturally graded, so you are allowed more time off for the death of a child living in the parental home than for the decease of an older child living away from home. Time off for weddings is graded according to the closeness of the relative being married. Of course there are variations from CAO to CAO with regard to the occasion of the entitlement. One CAO checked by Geddes in his study of Dutch management attitudes provided for a single day's leave if your brother was being ordained; another provided for time off for journalists if they were adopting a child (Geddes, 1990). But these variations are transcended by a pattern of explicit itemization, and it is detail of this kind that makes the CAO such a long and impressive document.

This explicitness with regard to entitlements has a wider interest in pointing to a difference between Dutch and British mentality and practice. Especially in such matters as minor entitlements to time off the British propensity is to keep it discretionary. A British supervisor or manager will like to keep such privileges within his or her gift, as a small control resource to induce conformity to the organization's needs, as a way to reward good employees. Such manoeuvring runs counter to Dutch notions of equality and dignity.

Finally, the CAO often provides evidence of Dutch high-mindedness, underlining obligations individuals must internalize and respect even if there is no sanction. So it is common to find a preamble in the form of *allgemene verplichtingen* (general duties or obligations). To take a specific example, Article 4, paragraph 1 of the 1988 CAO for Grolsch, the Enschede-based brewery, reads: *'De belangen van de werknemer als een goed werknemer te behartigen, ook indien geen uitdrukkelijke opdracht daartoe is gegeven.'* This clause underlines the obligation to act as a decent and conscientious employee even in the absence of any specifically allocated task, that is, to get on and do something useful. This mentality is again distinctively Dutch, with a touch of the Calvinist. Parodying only a little, the traditional attitude of the British employee is much more along the lines of we will do what we are paid for, and if you leave us loopholes, we will be free to exploit them.

A further point of interest when discussing industrial relations is that the Netherlands, unlike Britain at the time of writing (1991), has a formal system of co-determination or industrial democracy, a system which centres around the *ondernemingsraad* (OR for short) or works council.

The Works Council

Before entering into the formal details of the industrial democracy system a few signposting generalizations may be helpful. First, there is nothing in the Dutch constitution about co-determination, but the Netherlands has in fact a quite well-developed system; this is in contrast with countries such as Italy whose constitution waxes lyrical on the subject of co-determination but where nothing has been done in practice. Such contrasts are a minor source of pride to the Dutch. Second, there is something of a disjunction in the interest shown in co-determination in Britain and the Netherlands. Co-determination systems in other countries are always of interest to the British, since Britain does not have such a system, and, with the 1977 Bullock report quietly forgotten, it is not likely to introduce statutory co-determination in the near future unless there is a change in political leadership or such a system is made mandatory by the Economic Community (EC). In the Netherlands, on the other hand, co-determination is regarded as very much a 1970s phenomenon, and is not really a 'hot issue' in the late 1980s or early 1990s (the principal co-determination law dates from 1971). Dutch managers seem now to regard the OR (works council) in a family matter-of-fact way. The standard answer to questions about how the OR system is working is that in this company certainly the OR is sensible and reasonable, and members share a realistic appreciation of the economic situation in which the company is operating (this means the OR is not making difficulties in the policy initiative area). At the same time there is some interest in the system among Dutch academics. Not all the implications of the legislation have been worked through in practice, nor have all the available tactics and responses been rehearsed; indeed, there is significant current research on the workings of the system. Lastly, the OR system is one of those areas where I found a high level of disagreement among the people I interviewed, often getting quite different answers to quasi-factual questions such as: what sort of people put themselves forward for election to the OR?

The start of the system was the Works Council Act of 1950, which required enterprises with more than twenty-five employees to institute a works council. The catch is that they did not do it. It was found in 1967 that less than half of the companies which should have set up ORs had actually done so, and it is in fact the later 1971 Act that is the mainspring of the nationwide OR system as it is today.

In essence this 1971 Act endows the works councils with three sets of rights—to consent, to advise, and to receive information— as well as defining the constituency and the electoral and other procedures.

In a little more detail, the right to consent means that the entrepreneur needs the agreement of the works council to introduce, amend, or withdraw measures relation to:

- pension insurance, profit distribution, or savings schemes
- hours of work and holiday arrangements
- pay or job evaluation systems
- health, welfare, and safety regulations at work
- policies on appointments, promotion, or dismissal
- training
- employee appraisal
- complaints procedures
- treatment of young employees.

The right to advise means in practice that there are certain issues on which the views of the OR must be heard, whether or not the management is obliged to heed these views and whether or not the OR has any right of appeal against subsequent decisions counter to its expressed views. These issues include any management decision which may lead to:

- loss of jobs

- substantial changes in work, or the conditions or circumstances of employment
- termination of business activities or an important part thereof
- substantial retrenchment, expansion, or other alteration in the operating circumstances of the business
- change in the operating location(s) of the business.

The right to information has three main components. At the start of the OR's 'period of office' the entrepreneur is to furnish it with information on the legal status and formal structure of the company, Articles of Association, and names and addresses of owner, directors, and top managers. Second, every year the OR is to receive the financial statements, a personnel plan, and a social policy survey (what the policy has been, whether any changes are expected). Third, the OR should be given twice-yearly statements about past and anticipated business activities and past and anticipated results.

Election to the OR is by secret ballot. There is a prescribed nomination system which favours trade union members without giving them any exclusive right to become candidates, and of course the size of the OR (number of members) is directly proportional to the number of employees in the company. Large companies with many works/sites have separate ORs for each site, and also operate a tiered OR system with, for instance, a works-level OR, a divisional OR, and a head office council or, as the Dutch usually call it, a *centrale OR*.

The OR has to meet at least six times a year, the meetings are to be during working hours, and employers are generally enjoined in the legislation to do all they can in terms of amenities and facilitation to assist the functioning of the OR. In the 'old days' (before 1979) the managing directors themselves or other on-site chief executives would normally act as OR chairperson, usually with the company personnel officer acting as OR secretary. Not any more. Now management keeps out of OR meetings, and the OR members choose their own office-holders. Instead every OR meeting is followed by a corresponding meeting between the OR and top management, this follow-up meeting being known as an *overlegsvergadering.* These meetings are chaired alternately by the managing director and the OR chairperson. Issues which are covered by a CAO are not admissible as items of OR deliberation.

This in outline is the formal system, but of course it leaves out most of the interesting questions. It is worth raising some of these, even if it is not possible to give definitive answers. First of all, is the system accepted on the management side? It is a pertinent question from a British standpoint because management in this country has been unenthusiastic about co-determination throughout the post-war period.

Does Management Accept the Works Council?

It is almost certainly the case that the system is accepted, any criticisms or reservations being peripheral. All the Dutch managers I questioned about it spoke of the OR system in a fairly matter-of-fact way, any real problems that it might generate being putatively assigned to another time (the 1970s) or another place (the west of the country, especially Amsterdam where employees are generally regarded by employers as more 'Bolshie'). Only two management criticisms of the OR emerged in the research interviews I conducted. The first is that chairing/participating in the *overlegsvergadering* is a fairly arduous and time-consuming business, and you are generally quite pleased when it is over. The other criticism, more diffuse, centres on the representativeness of the OR, the implication being that if the OR were more representative you could use it for reliable upward and downward communication, and do deals with it which would stick. Thus I came across criticisms along the lines of:

- You think you can 'take the temperature' of the workforce via the OR, but they may inadvertently mislead you.
- Because you have the OR you neglect informal contacts with the workforce.
- The OR becomes a sort of barrier between you as management and the rank and file of the workforce.

One managing director recounted that he had conscientiously

negotiated with the OR a new summer holiday system which would be beneficial in terms of work output, only to have it rejected by the workforce after securing OR approval. The fact remains that there appears to be general acceptance of the OR, both in principle and in practice. The only stories I heard of flouting the OR and its various rights to advise and be informed concerned foreign-owned (American) companies operating in the Netherlands.

Who Becomes an OR Member?

The simple answer to this question is that it is employees who are 'organized', which means members of trade unions. The nomination system for OR membership does explicitly favour employees who are union members, while not excluding others. Indeed one of the few points of agreement amongst the Dutch interviewees was that most OR members are trade unionists, or at least that the typical OR member is 'organized'.

To digress for a moment, I have reason to believe from a systematic interviewing of German personnel managers that there is some further patterning of works council membership in West Germany. To put it pithily, the typical works council member in a German company is male, middle-aged (not young), German (not a *Gastarbeiter*, foreign worker), and above all skilled. I have often asked people in a position to know in the Netherlands if there is any patterning analogous to the German kind. The usual answer is no, the OR membership is a complete cross-section (and if not there is a good reason, such as there being no women employees in a particular company, or that none of the foreign workers speak Dutch) and so on. But there must be some doubt as to whether this is true, or whether these answers reflect a Dutch reluctance to confess to any departure from theoretical egalitarianism.

One thing that has emerged from such questions is that a Dutch OR may well include professionally qualified middle managers such as engineers and accountants. Where such people are among the members of any given works council they must surely increase its capacity to solve management problems if the council so wishes. That the OR should seek to assist management in this way is by no means out of the question. One *commissaris* (supervisory board member) I interviewed responded to a general question about the role of the OR by saying he was rather impressed with their contribution in his company. When pressed, he produced several good examples:

- The OR saw the need to reduce the number of hierarchical levels in the operating units to raise motivation (and was the cause of this policy being initiated).
- The OR suggested reorganizing the operating units of a company their company had acquired on a functional rather than a product basis (done to good effect).
- The OR is good on the financial analysis of the annual report presented to them, often suggesting new possibilities for the beneficial application of statistical analysis.
- The OR devised a new appeals system, whereby an individual at loggerheads with his immediate supervisor can appeal 'up-the-line' without undermining the chain of command.

Another interviewee suggested that where the professionally qualified manager or staff specialist becomes an OR member, the reason will not be so much a desire to find a new forum for the expression of managerial talent but rather a manifestation of a particular philosophic temperament. That is to say, such OR members will be distinguished by a thoughtful, serious-minded, socially responsible view of what the enterprise is engaged in and how to pursue its objectives. This characterization certainly fits my own observations.

Tactics

Co-determination law in any country is interesting not only for its content but also for the kind of tactics it facilitates on both sides. Consider the Dutch situation where the OR has both consent and advice rights. This opens up, at least in theory, enormous bargaining possibilities where the OR could trade off a consent against an advice concession, along the lines of: 'You take our advice not to close the (loss-making) works in Breda, and we will rubber-stamp your new employee appraisal system.' The possibility exists, the question is, do they do it?

Raising this issue with a number of academics and managers in the Netherlands the usual response was no, or not very much, or not yet. Again, I am not sure whether this reflects the naïvety or high-mindedness of Dutch OR members, or a reluctance to admit to a foreigner anything as discreditable as horse-trading. Another consideration voiced by some interviewees is that it is too soon: the current system was fine-tuned by legislation in 1979 and 1982 and both sides are still feeling their way, trying out the system, flexing their constitutional muscles. In any case a full tactical exploitation of the constitutional possibilities is unlikely in the current managerialist and cost-cutting climate of the early 1990s.

What do they Talk About?

Are any generalizations possible about the content of OR meetings, or more particularly the *overlegsvergadering* (the 'morning after' meeting where OR-rehearsed issues are presented to management)? Many respondents say there is no scope for generalizations, that each and every *overlegsvergadering* is different. But they do also say that on many issues managers have difficulty in conceiving a non-managerial viewpoint, or, even more, staff specialists develop tunnel vision, especially where their pet projects are concerned, and cannot anticipate the human implications of them. On such issues the OR input may be critical as an alternative version of reality largely inaccessible to corporate technocrats.

An alternative way of putting it is to say that the OR will seize upon, or emphasize, the social aspect of any phenomenon, which is probably the last thing in the mind of the (managerial) initiator of most schemes. One personnel officer, for intance, described how he presented to an *overlegsvergadering* detailed and comprehensive plans for a works training programme. He was proud of the construction of the programme, ready to hear criticism of the detailed content, and equally ready to defend his creation. In the event all the discussion was about the socio-occupational fate of those employees who opted not to participate in the training programme because they doubted their own educational readiness.

Another practical point that has been made about the *over-legsvergadering* is that it often ends with a *rondvraag*, the chairman going round the table asking those present if there is anything else they would like to raise. This is often the occasion for the raising of issues in rather emotional terms; the issues tend to be recent, unpredictable, and subjectively important for the delegate concerned. It is sometimes said ruefully that the *rondvraag* doubles the length of the meeting.

Another of the personnel officers interviewed had had an *over-legsvergadering* earlier in the week of the interview, and was able to summarize the agenda. This may be of interest as a practical example:

1. Presentation of company performance results to the meeting.
2. A joint discussion of the programme for quality improvement.
3. Problems with the *arbeidsinspectie* (in institutional terms, Department of Industry inspection; the FNV trade union confederation had condemned the industry concerned as generally dirty and unsavoury, with the result that there were frequent inspections resulting in endless censure measures and exhortations to change this and that on grounds of safety or improved conditions).
4. Investments, principally in new machines and production equipment.
5. Automation of part of the production process, and how this would make the company concerned the most advanced in the industry.
6. Price (reduced) of the company's main product to employees.
7. The following year's holiday arrangements.
8. The ATV (*arbeidstijdsverkorting* or shortening of the working week) system: progress in reducing the working week.

What Difference has it Made?

If the original (1950) Works Council Act was more honoured in the breach than in the implementation, the 1971 Act has been respected, which means that the Netherlands has had a proper works council system for getting on for two decades. Has it made any difference?

A number of answers to this question emerged in the interviews, only one of which has been canvassed so far, namely the view that the works council is not an issue (or threat), especially in the climate of the late 1980s or early 1990s. One issue that is intriguing is whether the operations of the works council raise opportunity costs for managers. Whether, that is, managers who would otherwise take initiatives or seek to implement what they see as desirable changes or bright ideas desist from doing so because of the need to justify such measures in the works council or defend them against counter-attack from that source. The suggestion here is not exactly that management may be emasculated, that it cannot initiate and implement, but rather that managers as individuals may be deterred from such actions by the anticipated hassle; in other words their opportunity costs may be raised. The answer to this question, uniformly received from Dutch managers, was no.

This response may be suspect not so much on a priori grounds, as because I have investigated a similar situation in Sweden where it is readily conceded that one effect of the works council–co-determination system is to deter many such management initiatives, to make them more 'hassle-ridden' and accordingly less attractive. So the possibility remains that the Dutch responses to this question reflect an unwillingness to admit (to a foreigner) any imperfection in the system. On the other hand, it may simply be different in the Netherlands. To be fair, the Swedish system, which basically gives the works council the right to decide nothing but discuss every-thing, does offer more scope for the frustration of managerial initiative. But there are other issues.

One is that the Dutch works councils have provided a distinctive viewpoint on issues and proposals. Whether or not Dutch man-agement (always) likes this viewpoint, it is not one they can 'manufacture' for themselves: you actually need to be a rank and file employee, and not a manager, to effect this interpretation, to see these (typically social) implications.

Perhaps the viewpoint professed most frequently by Dutch managers is that the existence of the works councils and their attendant rights conditions management's thinking, puts a caution on their proposals, and leads to a more reflective and conscientious approach to possible change. To put it crudely, it is much more likely that management will be asking itself: how will this look to the works council, will they see objections we don't see, is it possible to sell it to them, and if so how? Proponents of this view have on the whole suggested that it is a good thing, that it has induced a desirable element of humane realism, whereas previously intended initiatives were only evaluated in relation to question of how shareholders/the stock market would react.

A variation on this theme is to say that the coming of co-determination in the Netherlands has conditioned the choice/emergence of top managers, that the system is a barrier to the appointment to high office of confrontationist managers, of managers with a reputation as 'union bashers'. The candidate for the top position should have a clean sheet in this respect, not be an over (media) exposed hard-liner. Neither Michael Edwards nor Lee Iacoca would find favour in the Netherlands.

Finally, there is another consideration, one of epochal transition, though the phrase is perhaps too grand. The system of co-determination was largely conceived and implemented in the 1970s, a period different not only in mood but also in objective economic circumstances from the decade that followed. Firms in difficulties in the 1980s had to emphasize speed both in the market-place and in their production operation, flexibility, and the readiness to do anything for the (potential) customers, and to do it fast. All this pointed to a need for greater management control and ran counter to aspirations for employee control. A challenge for the 1990s will be to reconcile the gains of co-determination with the more competitive operational imperatives of the later period.

The Transfer of Undertakings

Merger and takeover activity increased generally in the 1980s with the USA and Britain leading the way. What is more, cross-border mergers have become more common, especially in the run-up to the Single European market (1992). What is not obvious in Britain and the USA is that these things are sometimes handled differently in other countries, not least in the area of employee rights. Whereas in Britain the transfer of undertakings, typically by transfer of share capital, is seen as essentially a financial affair, pretty well the exclusive concern of the financial community, such takeovers in the Netherlands are subject to some employee control and involvement. And again, employee rights in this matter are vested primarily in the works council.

The works council's right to be informed, to give consent, and to offer advice has already been mentioned. Corporate decisions that will have important social consequences for employees are subject to the works council's advisory provision, and such decisions include plant closures, expansion of company activities, major new investments, and of course takeovers. Such decisions may only be taken by companies when the works council has had the opportunity of expressing its opinion. What is more, if the works council feels a company has failed to do this it may appeal against the company decision to the Chamber of Undertakings of the Court of Justice in Amsterdam (*Ondernemingskamer van het Gerechtshof te Amsterdam*). And indeed in the course of the 1980s the Amsterdam Chamber of Undertakings did find in favour of the works council in a significant minority of cases, albeit on procedural grounds rather than with reference to the content of the corporate decision.

All this is a far cry from takeovers in Britain and the USA. An actual example of these processes in operation in the Netherlands may be helpful. The following illustrative case is taken from an Oxford University D.Phil. thesis (Wenlock, 1990). It concerns the firm of Nutricia, with its head office Zoetemeer, and Nutricia's subsidiary Preservenbedrijf in the southern town of Breda.

Nutricia is primarily a dairy produce manufacturer and provider of dietary products; it had acquired Preservenbedrijf in 1970. The latter, originally a jam factory, moved into the production of extruded potato snacks together with dehydrated meat and vegetables. By the mid-1980s Preservenbedrijf was the second largest snack food producer in the Netherlands and employed some 335 people at its Breda works.

In 1985 the Preservenbedrijf managing director brought the McKinsey management consultants into the company, with the prior knowledge of the works council of course, with the task of recommending new product and market opportunities that could sustain Preservenbedrijf's growth. In fashioning its recommendations the McKinsey report declared that Preservenbedrijf did not fit strategically into Nutricia's activities. In 1986 the Nutricia board in turn decided that Preservenbedrijf's business was indeed peripheral to its own strategic focus, and so Preservenbedrijf came to be up for sale.

The Preservenbedrijf employees were informed of this intention, and the first interesting development was that the works council produced its own set of conditions for the sale. These included a five-year guarantee for all employees, and the demand that there should be no dismantling of Preservenbedrijf by the new owner, no splitting it up into different parts or businesses, and that new investment should be made.

Still in 1986 the American company General Mills, with its headquarters in Minneapolis, bid for Preservenbedrijf via its Dutch subsidiary Smiths Food Group. Again the Preservenbedrijf works council was informed, and given details about General Mills and Smiths Food Group, regarding both their backgrounds and their intentions. At this stage the Preservenbedrijf works council engaged the services of an adviser, in fact a law professor, to assist them in making a recommendation on the General Mills takeover initiative; this move is in conformity with Dutch law, and the adviser was paid for by Nutricia, Preservenbedrijf's parent company.

In the event the Preservenbedrijf works council recommended against acquisition by General Mills. There was some doubt about the complementarity of the two companies, and therefore about the post-acquisition intentions of General Mills. Another fear was that Preservenbedrijf would end up as (merely) a subsidiary of Smiths Food Group in the Netherlands. There were also some question marks about the willingness of General Mills to co-operate with the works council at Smiths Food Group that did not augur well. The Preservenbedrijf works council's advice against General Mills settled the matter: the Nutricia board informed General Mills of the development, and General Mills withdrew their offer. Preservenbedrijf was on the market again.

The next bid for Preservenbedrijf came from the British company Dalgety. This was received more sympathetically. First, the intended acquisition was seen as consistent with Dalgety's policy of moving from agribusiness to food processing. Second, Dalgety already owned Golden Wonder, with Dutch and British operations, and there were no negative vibes in the Dutch case. Third, Preservenbedrijf saw the possibility that they would become raw material suppliers to Golden Wonder in Britain, thus expanding their operations. This time the works council recommendation was in favour, and Dalgety duly bought Preservenbedrijf from Nutricia in the summer of 1987.

This is not the kind of story one can read in the *Wall Street Journal* or the *Financial Times*. It shows Dutch law, practice, and values to be different. But this is not a simple tale of the virtuous Dutch morally downstaging the power-mongering British and Americans, as another bit of the story will make clear.

After the withdrawal of the General Mills bid and before the appearance on the scene of Dalgety the Nutricia management announced certain measures aimed at 'dressing Preservenbedrijf up for sale' (Wenlock, 1990). These included:

- maximizing Preservenbedrijf's sales
- a cost reduction programme
- an embargo on investment and training costs
- a moratorium on wage rises.

It is probably fair to see here some signal from Nutricia's top management to the Preservenbedrijf works council that Nutricia's intention to sell was a serious one, not designed to founder on a series of works council objections. In the final deal with Dalgety the works council's earlier demand for a five-year guarantee for all employees turned into a two-year guarantee, the works council conceding that two years was the norm—the dynamics of high-minded realism.

The Shop Floor

The burden of this chapter, with its focus on the formal, organizational, and even documentary—trade unions, negotiaton procedures, legislation, works councils, CAOs—will create the impression of an organized, legally protected, and formally participating workforce in the Netherlands. Such an impression is fair, but it carries a danger for some outside observers. The danger is that one might infer from the panoply of workers' rights and organizations that Dutch management has been emasculated, that its authority in the workplace is tenuous. This prompts the question: how disciplined or disorderly is the typical Dutch factory?

The first and obvious indication is the strike rate. The number of days lost through strikes in the Netherlands has always been low, even in the euphoric 1970s. Yet there is a view that strikes are simply the tip of the iceberg. Below this tip may be a welter of minor discontents and grievances, centring around such issues as supervision and work safety, conditions and supervision, sub-contracting and overtime, work allocation and discretionary reward, and much else of this ilk (Lawrence, 1984). Traditionally British industrial relations have been replete with incidents of a sub-strike level kind. What of the Netherlands?

The question is not susceptible to a definitive and quantified answer; it can be no more than a matter of experience and informed opinion. With this qualification it should be said that the Dutch workplace appears to be disciplined and orderly. If you ask blue-collar workers about their tasks and work situation their answers suggest that they assume at least a modicum of responsibility for the job: there is less moaning, less delegating of blame upwards, less looking for excuses for poor performance, more willingness to get things done and even to keep the place clean and orderly while doing them than you would expect to find in Britain.

Another way to probe this issue is to talk to production managers, and especially to ask them open-ended questions about problems and constraints. In the case of Dutch production managers this typically produces references to technical problems and to the organizational–technical parameters of production. It does not, interestingly, provoke any disquisition on the industrial relations climate or accusations of employee dissidence.

There is a certain paradox here. Dutch employees do have a sense of their rights and of what is owed to them. They are not supine, not willing to be imposed upon, exploited, or rail-roaded by employers. But this disposition finds expression in formal ways, in trade unionism, in the works council, and in the CAOs and the negotiation that precedes them. It does not appear to lead to the endless workplace friction that has been so much a part of the industrial tradition in Britain.

4

Where Dutch Managers Work

WHEN Americans and Britons think about the Netherlands as an economic entity there is a tendency to conceive of it as a smaller version of its neighbour West Germany: both are prosperous, export-led economies, both enjoying the reputation of being a 'clean, well-lighted place', both with enviable infrastructures. In fact the economy of the Netherlands probably has more in common with that of France, and traditional France at that.

Exports and the Shape of the Economy

Consider in this connection the comparative breakdown of exports from the Netherlands shown in the table below (while the figures are not recent, the pattern has changed little).

Proportion of Total Exports, 1980

	Netherlands	W. Germany	EC
Agriculture and food	22	5	11
Energy	22	–	7
Machinery	13	29	22
Vehicles	4	16	12
Other manufactured goods	35	42	43

Source: Tweede Kamer (Dutch House of Commons), *Export Nota*, 1981–2, No. 17532, p. 51.

Three simple points may be made straight away. First, the Netherlands are strong in energy exports. This derives in part from the discovery of substantial natural gas deposits outside the northern town of Groningen in 1958, with supplies coming on stream in the early 1960s. The other source of Dutch energy exports is petroleum refining. The Anglo-Dutch multinational Shell is the third biggest company in the Netherlands by workforce size (and the biggest by turnover) and Rotterdam, the world's largest port, is a major refining centre and home of the oil spot trade.

Second, the Netherlands enjoys relative strength in agriculture, of which more later, and is strong in a variety of food processing industries, including brewing, as we noted in Chapter 1.

Third, the Netherlands is not strong in heavy industry, or in traditional industries except chemicals, or in mechanical engineering generally. In all this it contrasts sharply with its neighbour West Germany. Even Philips, with its considerable range of electrical and electronic products, is characteristically not involved in the 'heavy end' of electrical engineering, that is, power generation and transmission equipment.

Nor is this uneven profile in manufacturing a necessary concomitant of the relative smallness of the country. Sweden, for example, with little more than half the population of the Netherlands, has a virtually complete range of manufacturing industry; it is well represented in mechanical and electrical engineering industries, as well as in chemicals, telecommunications, planes, and motor vehicles (Lawrence and Spybey, 1986).

It is also interesting that economic pride in the Netherlands does not focus narrowly on manufacturing expertise. Consider as an example the purchasing policy of Nederlandse Spoorwegen (NS), the Dutch railways. NS announced in the summer of 1989 its intention to acquire new rolling stock, in the form of 116 of the distinctive Dutch double-decker carriages, and 38 new locomotives. The locomotives were to be bought from the French, and the carriages from a company in Bad Aachen, West Germany (*De Volkskrant*, 25 July 1989). Imagine this happening in Britain, France, or Germany. What the figures presented at the start of the chapter conceal, however, is a variety of corresponding strengths including but not restricted to energy and farming.

Some Samples of Companies

In 1987 the journalist Susanne Piet published a fascinating set of interviews with some eleven Dutch entrepreneurs (Piet, 1987), though unfortunately the work is not available in English translation. Setting aside for a moment the style and character of these entrepreneurs as individuals, it is instructive to note the companies they represent. The little sample includes:

- oil trading
- two insurance companies
- a distribution company
- two banks
- Schipol (Amsterdam airport)
- a textile company
- a dairy products firm (Nutricia, discussed in Chapter 2)
- a brewery (Grolsch)
- another food-processing company (Douwe Egberts, producing tea, coffee, dry groceries, and confectionery, as well as tobacco and a range of personal care products, one of the household names of the Netherlands).

It is, quite simply, a list from which traditional industry is absent. A small sample, admittedly, and perhaps misleading since the author is picking entrepreneurs with a high profile as individuals rather than representative companies. Let us therefore look at the slightly larger sample of forty-nine companies from Henk Mulder's book surveying the pros and cons of Dutch companies as employers for qualified people coming into the labour market (Mulder, 1989). The breakdown by branch of industry of Mulder's sample is as shown in the table on page 68.

Mulder provides a decent sample of companies for a smallish country, though his selection may be a little skewed by his interest in companies likely to be chosen by graduates of university and HBO colleges—his work is actually entitled 'The 49 best companies to work for in the Netherlands'. He also leaves out Philips, presumably on the grounds that everyone knows exactly what Philips

Forty-nine Dutch companies by branch of industry

Branch of industry/economy	Number of companies
Financial services	7
Computers and software	7
Food and drink	6
Metal, glass, and plastics	6
Consultancy, advertising, and PR	4
Oil and chemicals	3
Graphics, paper, and office machines	3
Biotechnology	2
Retail and distribution	2
Trade and transport	2
Newspapers and publishing	2
Employment agencies	2
Recreation and real estate	2
Carpets	1
Total	49

is like and is familiar with its recruitment patterns—whole classes of graduating electronics engineers taken on 'at a stroke'. With this qualification it is probably a fairly representative selection: a small rump of traditional and metal products companies plus oil and chemicals, and then into banks, insurance, software, transport, real estate, consultancy, and advertising, together with the ubiquitous Dutch breweries and food products companies.

The biggest companies

KLM, in one of its publicity booklets, has assembled a list of the top twenty companies by workforce size as of 1987. It is a fascinating list (KLM, 1989):

1. Philips (electrical and electronic products)   341,567
2. Unilever (food and household products)   300,000

3. Shell (petroleum)	136,000
4. AKZO (chemicals)	69,000
5. Vendex International (mainly retailing)	52,000
6. Ahold (grocery chain)	35,748
7. Rabo (bank)	32,307
8. ABN (bank)	29,156
9. Heineken (brewery)	28,418
10. Hoogovens (iron and steel)	28,337
11. DSM (chemicals)	26,457
12. KLM (airline)	23,932
13. AMRO (bank)	23,714
14. Nationale Nederlanden (insurance)	22,691
15. Koninklijke Nedloyd Groep (shipping, transport)	22,266
16. SHV Holding (energy, transport, trading conglomerate)	21,900
17. DAF (trucks and cars)	14,748
18. Van Leer (packaging materials)	13,551
19. VMF Stork (engineering construction)	12,243
20. HBG (heavy construction)	11,993

This list is selected on the simple criterion of number of employees, a criterion likely to favour big manufacturing companies. Yet once again non-manufacturing enterprises have a signficant place. Some of the entries are quite remarkable. Vendex in fifth place has a number of interests, but the crux of it is the nationwide chain of Vroom and Dreesmann department stores. Ahold in sixth place is again primarily a retail operation in the form of the Albert Heijn grocery stores. Rabo is the biggest bank, with a history of lending to farmers, a Dutch Crédit Agricole. Less than a third of these top twenty companies are in the traditional or heavy industry sectors. It is an interesting and distinctive profile for a rich OECD (Organization for Economic Co-operation and Development) country.

Agriculture

It is clear that agriculture is important in the Netherlands, and it got a boost from the *ruilverkaveling* or government-sponsored enclosure movement in the 1960s. Dutch agriculture is also very versatile, including meats and cereals, as well as dairy and market garden produce (*Statistisch Jaarboek*, 1984). Even things that are difficult to get in the Netherlands, such as mutton, are often being produced for export.

Dutch agriculture is distinctive in being intensive and high-tech. As a representative of the Rabo Bank, the major lender to farmers, put it, 'Their financial needs are like those of industrial companies'. Indeed, Dutch farmers are always investing in technology and building—greenhouses, cowsheds, and barns, irrigation techniques, humidity and temperature control equipment, and of course computers.

Besides the usual range of agricultural produce, flowers and especially bulbs are important in the Netherlands. The Dutch rival the Germans as the great flower buyers of the world, and flowers are a significant export item. In his very positive account of Dutch life Frank Huggett has amazing tales of flowers picked in the afternoon, promptly packed, and flown out to appear for sale on the streets of New York City the following morning (Huggett, 1983). Indeed the tulip has become something of an emblem for the Netherlands; Dutch tulips turn up everywhere. When the Dutch government, for example, decided to move its embassy in Israel from Jerusalem to Tel Aviv—seen as a negative development by the Israelis, who want other countries to recognize Jerusalem as the capital—the Dutch–Israeli Friendship Group (ICN: Israel Comité Nederland) donated 800,000 tulips to Jerusalem to cheer up the disappointed citizenry (*Jerusalem Post*, 14 April 1990).

But Dutch agricultural products are not only important as a source of export earnings, and occasionally as national emblems. Dutch agriculture also fuels the food processing industry, and is sometimes the occasion of the Dutch propensity to engage in novel and complicated organizational forms, in this case agricultural co-operatives.

Co-operatives

In the late 1980s there were some sixteen to twenty agricultural co-operatives in the Netherlands (the number varies, and there is a trend towards amalgamation). Most of them are dairy produce co-operatives.

The typical set-up is something like this. A group of dairy farmers will own and be tied into a co-operative, to which they will deliver all their milk. In the case of the larger co-operatives these farmers will be numbered in thousands. The co-operatives then run factories for the manufacture and processing of dairy products, variously including cheese, yoghurt, milk desserts and puddings, milk powder, condensed milk, flavoured milk drinks, butter, and what in Dutch is called *consumptie melk*, that is, ordinary milk consumed in households.

In addition the larger co-operatives negotiate with retail chains such as Ahold, and with conventional, non-co-operative food product companies such as Unilever and Nutricia, for whom they may function as suppliers of raw materials and partly processed inputs. Again, the co-operatives, at least the more substantial ones, are engaged in research and development, marketing operations, and export initiatives. The manufacturing aspect may be substantial: one of the larger co-operatives, Noord Nederland, reported having thirteen factories in 1987, although it aimed to implement a rationalization programme over the 1987–91 period. Another of the larger ones, CCF (Cooperative Company Fricsland), runs manufacturing subsidiaries in Third World countries, sometimes locally sourced, sometimes sourced by recombining into milk exported residual fats and powder.

Running a Dutch agricultural co-operative is a tricky business, in all sorts of ways. One dynamic constraint concerns the quota system. The EC wishes to limit milk production, and has thus imposed quotas. These quotas, furthermore, are country quotas, so that the Dutch are precluded from buying other countries' quotas. The national quotas are then broken down, so that individual farmers each have a quota.

Now the co-operatives are interested in achieving volume, to obtain both economies of scale and an advantageous presence in the market-place. You would normally pursue this objective by encouraging the farmers to produce more milk, but this option is ruled out by the quota systèm. So the pursuit of scale proceeds in two other ways. Negatively, by keeping in the combine the farmers it already has. They are not allowed to leave, at least not without paying a substantial quitting fee; only when a farmer dies does the inheritor have the chance to 'renegotiate the contract'. But the positive approach is more important: the co-operative wants to grow, to attract in more farmers (and their quotas), and since there is competition between co-operatives, and from independent traders, the pursuit of scale leads to co-operatives trying to raise the price of milk, that is, to make its principal raw material more expensive. This is the reverse of normal industrial logic, where you seek to lower the price of raw material inputs (Lawrence and Lee, 1984).

The problematic may be put differently, and more broadly. Agricultural co-operatives are an instance of vertical integration, of placing under unitary ownership and control two stages in the value chain, in this case raw material provision and the production of goods. This situation always puts a strain on management; in the present case co-operative managers have to manage factories, farmers, and markets. This requires restraint and sophistication.

The situation is given a further twist by the organization and control structure of the co-operatives themselves. The usual arrangement is that all the farmer-members come together in a general meeting (*algemeeme vergadering*) akin to the shareholders' annual meeting of a public company. This meeting then elects a control committee (*bestuur*) from its own members, that is, composed of farmers. This committee then appoints, broadly controls, and may dismiss, the management team (*direktie*). So professional managers report to a group of elected farmers. Even given Dutch restraint this is bound to lead to tensions sometimes.

The dairy industry is undoubtedly competitive. In addition to the domestic competition just noted, there is stiff competition in export markets. There are some very desirable export markets, including many of the Arab countries which lack the pasture to supply their own dairy product needs but have money to spend. There is also fierce competition from New Zealand, unhampered by EC quotas, and to a lesser extent from Israel (Lawrence, 1990).

One advantage of farmer control in the co-operatives is that farmers see the production process in the foreground, and are ready to spend on it, not only on the farms themselves but on the co-operative's factories. The results of such investment may be a real source of pride. As a representative of one of the leading co-operatives remarked, 'Our cheese warehouse is the most modern in Holland, which means in the world'.

There is a possible downside in that farmers are inclined to neglect the marketing function. Yet the dairy industry is so competitive that you have to work hard to hold on to market share, and compete internationally for exports. Few of the processes in the dairy industry are energy-intensive (whey filtration is an exception), so energy savings are not a focus of research activity. Instead research and development is directed principally at new product development, the search for new cheeses, for instance, to stand alongside the immortal Gouda. The two focuses are branded consumer goods, for sale both at home and abroad, and selling milk to manufacturing companies as a product-specific raw material.

The whole enterprise is very Dutch, not only based on the national strength of agriculture but enshrining the Dutch gift for making complicated organizational forms work. What is more, it offers scope for that Dutch resourcefulness abroad illustrated in Chapter 1 by the overview of Heineken's operations. Who else but a Dutch co-operative would be successful in exporting fresh dairy produce to fast food outlets in the Far East?

Transport

The Netherlands is a transport paradise. It boasts the world's largest harbour, Rotterdam, and, as we have been, a shipping company (Nedloyd) is among the country's top twenty employers. There is also a substantial network of navigable rivers supplemented with canals, which accounts for 28 per cent of the movement of inland goods measured by ton-kilometres (Shetter, 1987). The rivers, especially the Maas (Meuse) and the Rijn (Rhine), cross international borders, so the waterways give the Netherlands an important stake in European commercial transport.

The same applies to the roads. Notwithstanding congestion in the *Randstad* (western conurbation), the country has an excellent road system; it is well endowed with motorways and well integrated with the European road system. This is especially true of the Twente area in Overijssel province by the West German border, where the A1 motorway from the *Randstad* articulates with the Münster, Hanover, and Hamburg–Scandinavia autobahns.

As you might expect, road haulage is a substantial industry in the Netherlands. There are seven or eight major hauliers, and some 2,000 smaller ones. There are two simple points to be made about the haulage business. The first is that it tends to be heavily computerized. The Dutch were quick to grasp the essential fact that everyone's lorries travel at much the same speed, so the key competitive weapon is the speed at which documentation is handled. The second is that Dutch road haulage is strongly European/international. Some of the Dutch hauliers, such as Frans Maas, have become household names in Britain, let alone the Netherlands. It is all part of the Dutch *élan* abroad outlined in the first chapter.

KLM is, in a sense, the world's oldest airline. It has existed continuously under the same name since its inception in the autumn of 1919—a claim that none of the other pioneering airlines can make. While domestic air transport is not very important in the Netherlands, KLM is strong as an international and especially intercontinental carrier. On one occasion in the late 1980s it was voted top airline; we will take up the KLM story in Chapter 9 to illustrate some Dutch business strengths.

Everyone likes the Dutch railways: the network is dense (Holland is one of the few countries which actually increased its rail network in the 1980s), and fares are cheap. As Shetter has pointed out, the entire Dutch railway timetable repeats itself every hour, and some portions every half hour (Shetter, 1987). Another feature of the Dutch railway system is that the Sunday timetable is much the same as the weekday one: English visitors find this particularly stunning. But it is the use rate in the Netherlands that is all-surpassing, at 69,000 passenger-kilometres compared with 48,000 in France, 31,000 in West Germany, and a mere 21,500 in Belgium. The NS (Nederlandse Spoorwegen—Dutch railways) runs 4,400 passenger trains daily, and it is claimed that 94.5 per cent of them arrive on time (Shetter, 1987). NS, with its headquarters in Utrecht, is in fact the country's second largest employer, after Philips (it is not shown on the KLM list quoted a few pages earlier, as this is a private sector listing).

Trading

The Netherlands undoubtedly has a strong trading tradition, consistent with its seafaring and colonizing past. We have already noted Dutch pre-eminence in oil trading, and some of the Dutch food processing industries are linked to commodity trading, for example in coffee, cocoa, and tobacco.

But the Netherlands is also the home *par excellence* of the import–export business, and it is worth probing the dynamics of this kind of operation with an example. Let us take the van Egmond company at Nijkerk near Amersfoort, which is small enough to understand in one go without a tediously long exegesis.

The van Egmond company originated as an agency in the Netherlands for fork-lift trucks made by the British company Lansing Bagnell. It traded successfully in this way until Lansing Bagnell embarked on direct manufacture in Benelux and had no further need of agents in that territory. This necessitaed a change of business for van Egmond, and by the late 1980s it was firmly established as a supplier of materials handling and internal transport equipment in the health care sector.

This means supplying the equipment that hospitals need to move goods and people around the premises—people to operating theatres and special treatment units, meals around the wards, debris out to the dustbins, visitors to and from the wards, clean linen in and dirty linen out, and so on. The actual stock-in-trade equipment is mostly trolleys and chairs and tubular frame tables, all of it purchased abroad, mostly from Finland and Sweden. Van Egmond acts as a supplier of such equipment and systems to the Benelux countries rather than just to the Netherlands, and at the time of my visit in the late 1980s was planning to extend its (sales) operations to West Germany as well.

Van Egmond is a success story, and it is possible to tease out some of the factors behind this success:

- It has achieved sole agent status for the foreign suppliers whose goods it buys, so it has no direct competitor in Benelux.
- This sole agent status is in part supported by paying suppliers within seven days (the Dutch norm is 30–60 days); even where this is done with borrowed money the prompt payment discount exceeds the interest paid.
- It has moved from equipment supply into consultancy, advising hospitals on their internal logistic needs, even at the hospital planning stage; this is the most critical development taking van Egmond into specialist fee-earning consultancy.
- It has extended the product range in order to offer customers a *complete* system so that they do not need to go anywhere else.

The whole operation bypasses the need for manufacture, and achieves a high turnover with a small workforce. In its blend of resourcefulness and customer care it is a very Dutch enterprise.

Software Companies

As is clear from the breakdown of Henk Mulders' forty-nine best companies cited earlier, software houses are well represented in the economy of the Netherlands. Indeed in the late 1980s some representatives of the industry spoke of it as growing at a rate of 30 per cent per year.

Side by side with any bias in the Mulder sample there is a structural reason for the plethora of independent software houses. This is that in high wage economies, with high social insurance costs per head of employee, and a high social–political emphasis on job security—and all these conditions are fulfilled in the Netherlands—employing organizations will tend to buy in services rather than establish in-house units to provide them. This tends to favour the growth of software houses and computer bureaux, as well as PR firms, advertising agencies, engineering bureaux, and consultancy firms in general. Exactly the same phenomenon is to be observed in Sweden, and for the same reason.

One point of interest is that given the overall shortage of programmers and systems design people many of these software houses employ expatriate British personnel side by side with Dutch staff (though this phenomenon is probably now past the peak). This means that some companies sometimes offer an interesting opportunity to compare Anglo-Dutch work attitudes among qualified professionals. On one occasion the differences were systematized for the author by the head of recruitment for one of the major houses, who characterized the British staff not only as cheaper in salary and social cost terms, but as more flexible—willing to work longer, to engage in overtime working, to accept any assignment (so long as it is well paid). This same source, not himself a Dutch national, noted that the Dutch are less concerned with salary levels, unwilling to work overtime (and want time off in lieu when they are coaxed into doing it), and do not want to be involved in professionally undemanding assignments even if such work is well paid. At the same time the Dutch are much more concerned about the intrinsic interest of the assignments, especially where these are seen to be associated with 'state of the art' technology; they like the idea that customer organizations will be illustrious, are very keen on training, and concerned about job security and pension provision, and even ask lots of questions at the recruitment interview stage about the company's hierarchy and structure. The Dutch were also seen as more concerned with rules and regulations generally and wanted everything spelled out.

It is not a static industry. In the late 1980s and early 1990s certain trends may be observed. First, there is a move, much regretted by the software houses, towards fixed contracts (as opposed to billable hours). Second, there is a desire on the part of the software houses to move as far up the customer's decision chain as is practical; to be able to start with the customer's need, problem, or challenge, that is, not with the customer's remedy specifications. Third, there has also been a growing humility/ practicality on the side of the system designers with regard to the information inputs needed to make the system work. 'In the good old days' system designers told end-users what was needed and left them to organize it: now there is more likely to be dialogue and an attempt by designers to enter into the practicalities of the users' world. And in an industry that has always seemed to transcend national borders there is now more working emphasis on 'Dutchness'. That is to say:

- Clients are increasingly likely to want to discuss their requirements in Dutch, even if they are fluent English speakers.
- The system arrangements have to take account of Dutch fears, the Dutch always being concerned that computerization will lead to unemployment.
- Dutch clients are wanting systems that accord with Dutch norms on privacy and discretion.

Perhaps one of the most interesting of the software houses in terms of organization and ethos is BSO, with its head office in Utrecht. Its top managers are keen to foster an entrepreneurial climate, to decentralize, to keep the staff as opposed to the line in their place, to restrict bureaucracy. The most important feature of BSO is the diversion of staff into independent cells of programmers. It works like this:

- The cells have up to 60–70 members (some 1,500 people work for BSO in total).
- The 60–70 members include a few who are staff (in terms of the line versus staff distinction) and this obviates the need for staff departments, considered a big plus by BSO management.
- Each of these cells has a general manager in charge of it, two sales people, and two field managers, so each cell is genuinely autonomous, having all it needs for effective operation within itself.

- The cells are also profit centres; they can spend what they like, and go for business on the open market.
- The drive to do well within this entrepreneurial climate is very motivating for the people who head the cells; as director Eckart Wintzen put it: 'It is an aggressive monster we have created'.
- The cell system is seen by BSO as producing 'genetic knowledge', as people move from cell to cell.
- With the expansion of the cells, and the number of cells, promotion chances are good.

But perhaps the best testimony to the effectiveness of the BSO system was in the form of a comment by the managing director's secretary, in a conversational space which an English person would have used to say something about the weather, to the effect that 'People find it stimulating to work here'.

The Banks

As in Britain, but in contrast to the USA, the main banks in the Netherlands have nationwide branch networks. They are, however, unlike British banks in that cheques, except Eurocheques, are little used, so the main Dutch banks are not primarily clearing banks in the British sense. Money transmission in the Netherlands, especially in the sense of paying bills and debts, is typically handled rather differently. Instead of writing cheques you fill in a written form instructing your bank to pay a certain sum to a certain recipient by transferring the money directly to the payee's account. You tend to do this form-filling in batches, and then take a pile of them into the local branch or mail them to the bank. These forms are blue, and are colloquially known as *blauwtjes* (little blue things).

Surprisingly in a country that prides itself on the absence of status differences, the main banks in the Netherlands are probably more differentiated by customer base than is the case in Britain. If you take the big four British banks—National Westminster, Barclays, Midland, and Lloyds—there are differences in the relative proportion of A and B customers (those in the higher socio-economic groups) but the differences are not large or obvious and the general public is largely unaware of them. The patterning seems to be stronger in the Netherlands.

In the Netherlands ordinary people use the Postbank, its facilities conveniently available at the nation's chain of post offices. Middle-class personal customers use ABN and AMRO, as do medium-sized and larger corporations. Small businesses, self-employed people, and above all shopkeepers use NMB, while RABO has its traditional strength in the rural areas and is the bank *par excellence* for farmers, as noted in the earlier sketch of Dutch agriculture.

One thing that the Dutch banks have in common, however, is that they are all strategic sites for the study of Dutch privacy and decency norms. Whenever Dutch banks conduct surveys of customer satisfaction or implement customer care programmes this comes up. You will be told, for example, that customers welcome the introduction of a queuing system, not so much because it is fairer but because it eliminates the possibility of another customer standing immediately behind you at the counter and perhaps overhearing your business. Again, it is said that Dutch personal customers welcome the idea of a personal banker, that is, dealing with only one person at the branch for all services, as this obviates the need for several branch employees to discuss the customers' affairs among themselves.

Another common characteristic of Dutch personal customers is a general enthusiasm for automation, especially for cash dispensers and ATMs (automatic teller machines). At the time of writing (spring 1990), ATM penetration is somewhat lower in the Nether-lands than in Britain, and very much more recent—almost exclus-ively a phenomenon of the late 1980s. This is currently seen as an important weapon in the competition for customers.

AMRO (Amsterdam–Rotterdam Bank) and ABN (Algemene Bank Nederland) are the two that are most like the big four banks in Britain, and most like each other. Both are the result of earlier amalgamations, particularly intricate in the case of ABN (Bosman, 1983). As noted, both have a largely middle-class personal customer base, including a good share of wealthy individuals. They are bankers to the bigger and better Dutch companies, and especially to the multinationals.

These banks have tended to raise the proportion of university or HBO qualified staff among their workforce. The proportion of HAVO school leavers joining these banks has also gone up significantly in the 1980s, while the MAVO proportion has gone down (see Chapter 2).

There is also a regional tinge to AMRO and ABN, at least in terms of their corporate customers. In his second book on the nature and connections of the Dutch élite, Jos van Hezewijk observes that AMRO originated in Rotterdam so you would expect it to have the accounts of more than its share of Rotterdam-based companies, but this is not the case (Hezewijk, 1988). Conscious that his finding will be puzzling to Dutch readers, used to the idea propounded in Chapter 2 that regionalism matters in the Netherlands, Hezewijk goes on to explain that AMRO has a subsidiary that originated in Amsterdam, and that if you cross-tabulate the location of corporate customers with AMRO and its subsidiary separately, then the regional affiliations you would expect as a good Dutchman are indeed realized. Symmetry is also preserved by Hezewijk's finding that in this matter ABN is a mirror image of AMRO—originating in Amsterdam but with a Rotterdam-based subsidiary (Hezewijk, 1988).

AMRO and ABN are of course rivals, and their rivalry was dramatized in one *cause célèbre* of the 1980s, the great Elsevier–Kluwer takeover battle. Leading publisher Elsevier, backed by AMRO, made a hostile takeover bid for the other leading publisher Kluwer. The response was that Kluwer, backed by ABN, merged with publisher Wolters to become Kluwer-Wolters and too big to be taken over by Elsevier. Actions of this kind are less common in the Netherlands than in Britain or the USA, but they make more impact and are talked about longer. All this traditional rivalry has been superseded, however, by a proposed merger. In March 1990 AMRO and ABN announced their intention of merging. At the time of writing (spring 1990) the merger has yet to be approved by the Ministry of Finance and the trade unions. The latter are likely to be unenthusiastic: AMRO and ABN have overlapping branch networks, so a merger is likely to lead to closures and redundancies. On the other hand, the merger can be justified in terms of relative size: the ensuing bank will be something like the tenth largest in Europe and the seventeenth in the world.

NMB (Nederlandse Middenstands Bank) is the bank with the strongest image, and the one most often in the news at the end of the 1980s. Its shopkeeper–small business affiliations are legendary. Henk Mulder's chapter on NMB is replete with phrases such as *'een bank voor slaggers en bakkers'* ('a bank for butchers and bakers') and *'bank voor de kruidenier op de hoek'* ('bank for the grocer shop on the corner') (Mulder, 1989: 214). NMB have also run the slogan *'de bank die met u meedenkt'* ('the bank that thinks with you'). The British general public are rather more hardened to appeals of this kind, after years of 'the listening bank', 'the action bank', 'the bank that likes to say "yes"' and so on. But such punchy little slogans are less common in the Netherlands, and *de bank die met u meedenkt* really caught on. I was told by an NMB representative that a survey showed NMB had achieved a corporate awareness with the Dutch general public second only to Heineken.

These, however, are not NMB's only claims to fame. Unlike AMRO and ABN it has grown from within, not by amalgamation. In contrast to the other two it has the reputation of being the bank where you can do well in management with the HEAO qualification (a particular version of HBO described in Chapter 2) as opposed to a university degree. It is also known for paying its middle managers well, a fact connected with its internal growth. In terms of ethos it is rather proud of its down-to-earth and energetic image—less deferential than the other two, allowing managers more independence, less likely to worry about deviations from convention so long as results are achieved.

The NMB head office in is Bijlmer, a satellite office block township in south Amsterdam. It is a distinctive building, irregularly shaped and departing from the conventional straight vertical and horizontal line normal in office buildings. The effect of these sloping walls and tilting roof lines is enhanced by edges picked out in an attractive blue. This head office is fairly new, and has been much talked about. But the biggest NMB story is their acquisition in 1989 of the Postbank, which it bought from the PTT or Dutch Post Office. The Postbank has some 5 million personal customers, and outlets at the country's 3,000 post offices. Its customer base is complementary to that of NMB, with its small business customers. NMB and Postbank together are bigger than all the other banks in the Netherlands except RABO.

This NMB–Postbank deal was only finalized at the end of 1989. While there is a plausible business strategy logic for the acquisition, it is too soon to say how well integration will be achieved. There are considerable differences between the two organizations, going beyond a difference in their customer base. Postbank has employed a lot of staff with relatively humble educational qualifications doing fairly routine transactions for a mass personal customer market. They are a disciplined staff, for whom routines and procedures count. The NMB staff, on the other hand, are more independent, better educated, and to a large extent attuned to discretionary dealings with small business customers. It is something of a clash in corporate cultures.

RABO is a federation of co-operative banks, originally founded on the Raiffeisen (co-operative) principle imported from Germany in the late nineteenth century. In the early days there was a plethora of little credit co-ops in both the north and south of the country. Eventually the need for some central services led to the establishment of a northern HQ in Utrecht and a southern HQ in Eindhoven. Then in 1972 these two merged to form Rabobank Nederlands (RN), also with its head office in Utrecht.

The structure is rather complicated. There is an AGM (annual general meeting) in Utrecht attended by getting on for 4,000 delegates, including a manager and two other staff from each branch. This AGM elects both a *raad van toezicht* (supervisory board) and a *raad van beheer* (control board), and the latter in turn appoints a *hoofd direktie* or central administration. This *hoofd direktie* in Utrecht is responsible for developing general policy, for new product development, and for developing common systems. But the enterprise is rather less directive than is normal in bank organization.

While RABO is renowned as the farmers' bank, and does indeed hold 90 per cent of the nation's agricultural account, this is by no means all. At the end of 1989 a RABO representative told the author that RABO has

- 40 per cent of all savings deposits in the Netherlands
- a substantial share of the small and medium-sized business accounts (the classic NMB area of operation)
- a 25–30 per cent share of the house mortgage market
- more ATMs than all the other Dutch banks.

It is also responsible for 45 per cent of all money transmissions in the Netherlands (cheques and *blauwtjes*), and is the country's largest supplier of travel services.

RABO is also AAA rated; this triple A is the most favourable rating for borrowing in international money markets. Only about 10–12 banks in the world share this rating (including National Westminster in Britain), and RABO is the only Dutch bank so rated. In short RABO has a low profile, but considerable substance.

The Multinationals

Again responding to the title of this chapter, a disproportionate number of Dutch managers work for multinational companies. As one of the smaller countries of Europe the Netherlands is unusual in having such a panoply of multinational companies. And it should be underlined that these multinationals are Dutch companies; they are not other people's multinationals 'camping out' in the Netherlands.

The lustre that the multinationals bestow on Dutch business life is heightened by the fact that several of them rank high by world standards, not just by Dutch or even European ones. So, for example, Shell is one of the leading oil companies in the world, Heineken is the world's third-largest brewery, Philips is in the world top ten electronics companies by size and will probably rank higher by research spending, and KLM is universally acknowledged as a leading airline.

The Dutch multinationals are important in various ways. Clearly they reinforce the international orientation of the Netherlands. In particular, the fact that two of them—Royal Dutch Shell and Unilever—are Anglo-Dutch gives Britain and the Netherlands something of a special relationship. Indeed you are always coming across company ownership and business links between the two countries. Nutricia, for example, owns Cow and Gate in England, and in turn is partly owned by Unigate; Dalgety, as we saw in Chapter 3, became the proud owner of Preservenbedrijf of Breda; Stanley Thornes, the British educational publisher, is part of Kluwer-Wolters.

Again there has been what one interviewee called 'a good spin-off of attitudes' from the multinationals. The lustre of the multinationals is good for Dutch economic pride, widens the horizons of the possible, makes large-scale operations in a small country seem viable, encourages a positive attitude to exporting, and so on. It is also sometimes argued that the presence and needs of the multinationals have contributed to the rise of a sophisticated banking system.

It has to be said that the existence of these multinationals raises several quite important questions, that for the most part cannot be answered—the data are incomplete, the phenomenon is not quantifiable, or there is simply a haze of conflicting opinions. Consider, for instance, the effect of the multinationals as exemplars of best management practice, as a powerhouse of management professionalism; are they serving to raise management standards nationwide? There are two answers. The first answer is that they have no influence, because no one ever leaves the multinationals (though a few make a one-way trip in after some work experience elsewhere). This view finds support in my experience from the tendency of the Dutch to compartmentalize into multinational and others. Tell a manager in a medium-sized company how they do it in Philips and he shows as much interest as if you had told him about current executive practice in Malawi.

On the other hand, there is also the view that the multinationals do have considerable influence; they are like management universities in action, their members ever present at functions and conferences, happy to give a seminar at the drop of briefcase. And this, too, has some truth in it. The multinationals keep 'popping up' in the Netherlands; whatever happens, they are represented at it; and you are also told that willingness to participate in seminars, conferences, and so on, is seen as one of the hallmarks of the promotable young multi-executive. At the end of the day, it is a difficult balance sheet to draw.

The relationship between the government and the multinationals is also somewhat controversial. While critics of big business deplore the presumed influence of the multinationals on the government, some representatives of the multinationals themselves say, more in sorrow than in anger, that with a 'trigger-happy' left-wing media, and an ever-watchful public, the multinational is never allowed to do what it wants (like closures) anyway. But the predominant view is that the multinationals do have influence, are listened to by government, and have regular contact with government. Jos van Hezewijk again demonstrates some top-level contacts between leading companies and political parties, especially the ever-present coalition partner the CDA (Hezewijk, 1988).

But perhaps most controversial of all is the role of the multi-nationals as subcontractors. Again, there are two strands of thought on this. One view—and one not espoused exclusively by representatives of the multinationals themselves—is that they spend vast amounts on subcontracting work. And because of their size and importance they raise standards wherever they go, checking out and improving the costing, methods, and quality control of their suppliers. The alternative view is: forget it, the multinationals are omnicompotent; whatever they want comes from within. The only time I put it to the test at one works of a multinational company I was told that half the components that went into final assembly came from without; it then turned out that half of that half actually came from other divisions of the same multinational, and only a quarter of the whole from independent suppliers. Again, you do not know how to draw a balance sheet.

It is also worth asking whether the multinationals cream the managerial labour market? It is quite clear that the multinationals are very attractive employers, though many Dutch people I spoke to denied any creaming effect. Their counter-argument was along the lines that lots of people think a small company will be more fun or offer faster promotion or more responsibility, so they do not join the multinationals. This is a perfectly reasonable claim, yet there are reasons to suspect creaming:

- The multinationals hire large numbers of graduates fresh from university and HBO colleagues; some respondents speak of them 'taking out' whole years of graduates *en bloc*, though this may be picturesque exaggeration.
- The multinationals get a second 'bite at the cherry' recruiting qualified people at a later stage with a few years' experience with other employers, though this seems to be a one-way traffic.

Do the multinationals pay more? It is a simple question but no one seems to know the answer. Typical answers are: yes, no, that is not the point! What then is the attraction of the multinationals? It would be an exaggeration to speak of consensus, but the most common answer is: security and pensions. And putative lack of security is the reason most often given for avoiding the medium-sized and smaller companies. Other attractions of employment in a multinational, mentioned by people I interviewed, include:

- prestige
- possibility of an international career
- possibility of changing functions and having wide job experience, without leaving the company (there are normative constraints on inter-company mobility in the Netherlands that will be explored in a later chapter—you can have it both ways in a multinational)
- pensions (no one seems to know or care if the multinationals pay well, but everyone is agreed that they are good pension providers).

Furthermore, and rather unexpectedly, the presence of the multinationals may actually serve to discourage entrepreneurialism. Part of it is that the multinational career option, with its emphasis on economic safety, pension, and calculable progress through a large organization, tends to accentuate the antithesis between entrepreneurialism and security. And at a more obvious level multinationals may be excluding competition. In this vein I once asked a Philips's manager if there were any rivals to Philips in Holland and was told yes, IBM!

Finally, the presence of the multinationals connects with the Dutch ability to adapt to and work within organizations with complicated structures. This ability to relate to the organizationally complicated has already been noted at several points. This talent is not caused by the multinationals, but is deployed to effect within them.

5

Management is not an Island

MANAGEMENT activity is focused on a task that is universal, and understood in terms of universal concepts—competitiveness, efficiency, profitability, and so on. Yet managers as people bring different things to this task: different assumptions, predilections, and tendencies. Some of this variation is of course purely individual. But the variation in terms of socio-cultural factors associated with particular countries leads to stronger and more consistent patterning. An important part of the answer to the question, what is Dutch management like, will be in terms of what the Netherlands as a society is like, and what are the general values and convictions of Dutch people.

To this end some salient features of Dutch society were outlined in Chapter 2, including *verzuiling* and the Calvinist legacy, regionalism, the political and education systems. We noted that *verzuiling* and regionalism together have implications for worker mobility and manager recruitment, that the Calvinist legacy underpins the Dutch aversion to bribery. In considering education, and particularly the political system, we hinted that the articulation, controls, and balances find a reflection in business life, in the co-determination and collective bargaining system explored in Chapter 3. The present purpose is to take these ideas a little further as a part characterization of Dutch management.

Vloeken is Aangeleerd

In the early 1990s the railway stations of the Netherlands were liberally adorned with posters depicting a virulent green parrot, poised menacingly above the slogan *vloeken is aangeleerd* ('swearing is learned behaviour'). These posters were put up by the *Bond tegen het Vloeken* (the Anti-swearing Association). There are two points of interest here. First, you could not readily imagine such a phenomenon in Britain, France, or the USA, albeit for different reasons. Second, note the terms of the condemnation—not just swearing is bad, or you should not do it, or it may give offence to others. But swearing is *learned*. You had a choice, you swearers; nobody made you swear, but you took the trouble to learn swear words and then went forth and used them. There is no cop-out here; the individual is stuck with moral responsibility, and behaviour is what we are going to be judged on.

This is again part of the Calvinist legacy that pervades Dutch society. But whatever the origin, the message symbolized by the green parrot is clear: be responsible, you will be judged. It is a serious business being Dutch. Of course in the late twentieth century it may well be society rather than God that holds you to account, but the principle of accountability is none the less paramount.

It shows in all sorts of ways, and not withstanding the tendency of mutual admiration of the Dutch and the British there are Anglo-Dutch contrasts here. The Dutch are not naturally flippant, or whimsical. These are characteristics of the amoral English, more concerned with effect than responsibility.

The Dutch take facts seriously. Not to do so would be to set yourself above the law. In his provactive critique of Dutch society, Derek Phillips, expatriate American sociology professor working in Amsterdam, attacks even Dutch higher education as being fact-driven. The most awful thing a Dutch professor can do is get a fact wrong (and the second most awful thing is to admit to not knowing a relevant fact). The Dutch like to praise in the same terms in which they blame. A good lecture, talk, or book will thus be represented as giving reliable information, even if its real merit lies in something else.

What is more, accuracy should be garnished by verifiability. Dutch transactions are not fudged, but written down, soberly recorded, as with the collective agreements (CAOs) discussed earlier. Another illustration which brings out the Anglo-Dutch contrast nicely is the Ph.D. examination. In England awarding a Ph.D. is something that tends to happen behind closed doors.

Someone who has power within the system defines a topic as viable, a candidate as suitable, and a projected output as a potential contribution to original knowledge. When the suitable candidate has completed the contribution the sponsor finds another suitable person to examine it; the three of them talk about it in a civilized way in a smallish room, and then give the candidate a doctorate.

Dutch practice is a little different, culminating in the *promotie*, or promotion of the candidate. The thesis is printed and circulated before the event, the occasion is public, the candidate performs on stage (not in an armchair) and responds to a series of questions from a battery of examiners before an audience.

Clearly there is a ritual element in the Dutch *promotie*, yet it is significant that the ritual has this content. After all, if something is serious, it should be treated responsibly. Only the English have developed the knack of treating serious things with a lightness of touch while embalming the trivial with mock gravity.

The Calvinist Legacy

In some instances Calvinist norms may quite literally inform workplace behaviour. A nice example is proffered by Henk Mulder in his discussion of the forty-nine best Dutch companies to work for (Mulder, 1989). The company concerned is Polynorm, which manufactures a variety of components for the building and automobile industries. Mulder quotes Wil Ledel, manager of the building products division, to the effect that 'The social control of a strong *gereformeerd* [strict Calvinist, see Chapter 2] population, such as exists in the village, does not stop at the factory gate. If anyone swears at work he must be censored and dealt with' (Mulder, 1989: 240). Or again, one of the foremen comments: 'There will still be no football played on Sunday and the swimming pool stays shut' (Mulder, 1989: 241).

But more often than not it is a case of the Calvinist legacy informing values rather than controlling behaviour. One manifestation of this is quite simply a celebration of honesty. In discussing Content Beheer, an employment bureau, Mulder quotes sales manager Paulien van der Harst on the subject of the job descriptions that Content agrees with would-be employing organizations: 'In this activity we are really honest, we won't report categorically the job is so great ... Honesty is the basis for the trust that we have to have in this branch' (Mulder, 1989: 69).

Material self-indulgence, of course, is not favoured. In his portrait of the computer systems firm Geotronics, Mulder quotes from the maintenance and installations director on the subject of (largely absent) fringe benefits: 'Company cars are strictly tied to function and the nature of the work'; 'Anything that tends towards the discretionary we seek to exclude'; 'In this company there is absolutely no hint of luxury and none can arise' (Mulder, 1989: 114).

Steadfastness is another Calvinist value that finds expression in management motivation and behaviour. Mulder's interviewees emphasize the long term, the virtues of persistence and commitment. In introducing the planning and real estate enterprise Heidermij, Mulder refers to the sporting record of its managing director Frank Schreve, who is chairman of the Nederlandse Sport Federatie (Dutch Sports Federation). Schreve's personal sport enthusiasm is climbing—and it has taken him to some of the peaks in the Andes. Schreve observes: 'That too is a question of endurance and completion' (Mulder, 1989: 128).

As a variation on this theme I was once told by a director of a transport company that they had established a modest presence in China in the 1970s, though it did not seem to be an especially profitable initiative. But the purpose was to show long-term commitment, to be seen to stay the course, not to be a commercial quitter; when China took off economically such corporate steadfastness would have its just reward.

The same idea runs through the Mulder account of the consultancy firm McKinsey, where the importance of long-term, stable business relationships is emphasized.

The turnover of McKinsey in the Netherlands is not published. But it is well known that around 90 per cent of this turnover comes from repeat assignments from existing clients. The bureau [McKinsey] is established there as a house [internal] adviser. This alone naturally tells you something about its reputation (Mulder, 1989: 185)

Sometimes the principles of right conduct are formalized. In his account of Océ, the photocopier and office automation equipment firm in Venlo, Mulder's first observation is that it was 'One of the first enterprises in the Netherlands with a "social statute" in which the rights of the employees were codified' (Mulder, 1989: 231). In one period Océ had surplus manpower, but 'collective redundancy just doesn't fit the culture of the company.' Instead Océ temporarily lent some eighty employees to other companies in the neighbourhood it wished to help. Océ manager Noud Immers feels that this is unique. One feels the company is entitled to this pride.

A Strain to Conformity?

The constraints that we are considering here are of course normative not legal. In practice it often seems as though the good Dutchman

- wants to conform;
- does not want to set himself apart, and thinks it is wrong for other people to do so;
- certainly eschews eccentricity;
- thinks it is wrong to make (invidious) distinctions between people;
- and probably does not believe in 'centres of excellence', individual or institutional.

One manifestation is that there is more ritual in Dutch life, even in social life. The elements of entertaining and extra-familial visiting, for example, are more patterned than in Britain. You know what an occasion is going to be like in the sense of being able to predict the form if not the content. And perhaps related to this is the presence of various homely conformity rituals. For example, the eve of St Nicholas' Day (5 December) is celebrated in the Netherlands: there is extensive gift-giving, and the gift has to be accompanied by a poem, in rhyme, or written according to an understood formula. School classes do this in an organized way. The interesting thing is that it is not a situation where the individual earns credit, but 'marks may be taken off' for failure to get it right. Several Dutch managers I interviewed themselves suggested this idea of restricted individuality, usually in giving explanations of other phenomena, such as lack of careerism, standardized executive remuneration, lack of interest in foreign management ideas, lack of executive mobility, and so on. People also quoted proverbs and sayings to express or substantiate points they were making, and it soon became clear that Dutch is a little treasury of proverbs condemning vanity, ecccentricity, and needless risk-taking. There is an exact equivalent of 'pride comes before a fall' in Dutch as in German, but it does not end there. The Dutch also have *naast je schoenen lopen* ('to walk beside your shoes'—say, to be too big for your boots) and the picturesque *hoog te paard sitten* ('to sit too high on your horse') clearly a condemnation of overweening pride with seigneurial overtones. But the vanity which feeds on the mindless praise of others, even more reprehensible, finds expression in *over het paard getild zijn* ('to be lifted *over* the horse'), indicating that the individual who wilfully surrenders to sycophants will not even get into the saddle. Neither does the wise man (good Dutchman) take unnecessary risks, a thought captured in the exhortation *steek niet je hoofd boven het maaiveld* ('don't put your head above the trench'). Yet perhaps the most telling of these proverbial exhortations is the oft-quoted *als je gewoon doet doe je al gek genoeg* ('when you act normal, that's already crazy enough'). Now depending on your point of view the genre can be viewed as proper censure of (some particular) human weaknesses, or as seeking protection in conformity. Is normal behaviour really that crazy, or does it do us good to think so?

Another pointer is the Dutch response to the popular and influential 1980s book *In Search of Excellence* (Peters and Waterman, 1982). In this the authors use a group of middle-term financial performance criteria to pick out top-performing American companies, which they then seek to characterize, that is, to say what is different and interesting about them and hopefully to explain the high performance. The book is well known in the Netherlands, and a Dutch translation is available. What is interesting is the widespread rejection of the idea and characterization of excellence.

The Dutch attack the book methodologically, which is admittedly rather easy to do. They also quote with relish the 'Who's excellent now?' argument, that is, they make play with the fact that some of the Peters and Waterman companies subsequently got into difficulties. When pressed Dutch managers tend to say that they do not like the idea of some companies being selected and differentially labelled, they do not like the conscious élitism of it all; if some of these companies subsequently fail, it is no more than they deserve, they should not have let themselves be 'lifted over their horse'.

Again, when pressed some interviewees pointed to the moral or psychological need to condemn those who sought the distinction of excellence but came unstuck. A popular example proffered by one manager concerned the very talented footballer Johan Cruyff. When Cruyff passed his prime as a player he went into running a training school for would-be champions, but with only mixed results. The press, so went the testimony, were quick to pick this up and label Cruyff as the 'so-called master' and an '*ex*-champion'. Another illustration given was an industrial achievement prize given to the head of the Fokker aircraft company, Frans Swarttouw. After the award it was discovered that a deal he claimed to have effected with a larger (American) company had fallen through, with serious results. What he is remembered for is the braggardly claim, rather than his successful rescue and turnround of Fokker.

But this proclivity also works the other way round. Everyone has the right not to be censored or condemned (unless and until they forefeit this by some act of overweening pride). This often emerged in discussions with personnel managers in Dutch firms, who are charged with selection, recruitment, management development, maybe even picking people out for 'high-flyer' programmes. The Dutch are never quite happy with this. One manifestation of this moral unease is the way Dutch personnel managers will tell you the recruitment criteria, and then qualify them: 'We like graduates with an average grade of 8 (6–9 are all pass grades, 9 being the highest)—but of course there is sometimes a good reason why someone has a lower average grade.' Or: 'We like people who completed their university course in 4–5 years; we don't turn them down if they took longer but they need to have a good explanation.'

Selecting people for high-flyer programmes is regarded as especially invidious. Again a manifestation of this is the zeal with which the personnel manager espouses the late developer syndrome. It goes like this: 'We pick most of them during their first six months with the company, but there are bound to be others whose merit shows at a later stage—you cannot always tell quickly.'

An easy test of this Dutch reluctance to judge comes from asking representatives of companies that recruit significant numbers of graduates if there are any particular universities they favour. This typically provokes a haughty negative, or if some patterning is conceded this is admitted to rather shamefacedly. There is an interesting contrast here with British personnel managers, who will make no bones about listing their favoured universities, often with highly stereotypical justification.

The same theme of refusing to judge between individuals is taken up by Derek Phillips. The higher education system, he suggests, is designed to mask differences in individual ability, and when differences appear they tend to be explained circumstantially. Or again, if something is at fault in an organization, the response will be to reorganize, to reform the system, not to deal with poorly performing individuals (Phillips, 1985).

In the same spirit the Dutch seem not to like generalizations. Although as a matter of definition generalizations do not make nasty individual comparisons, they carry with them a touch of arrogance. The person making the generalization implicitly claims detachment, is looking down on that entity which is the subject of the generalizing. It is a kind of setting yourself apart, a new thought crime.

This tends to put the foreign enquirer in a bit of a quandary, since an obvious way to learn about a country is to ask people who ought to know about whatever it is that interests you, and then recycle the more interesting propositions in subsequent discussions to check them out. This invariably provokes denial, a qualifying of the proposition, or at best grudging acquiescence. It is not the content of the proposition that is objectionable. Denial is just as likely for propositions of praise as for critical ones. It is the act of generalizing which is viewed with distaste. It runs counter to Dutch humility, and to the Dutch spirit of fair play. You should not generalize about people because you may be doing an injustice to some exception or minority or special case you have not thought of. A Dutch person will help you think of it.

The Distaste for Status Differences

At a practical and organizational level the proclivities discussed above lead to a low tolerance of status differences. This is a leitmotiv of the Mulder interviews. The Buhrmann-Tetterode company (diversified enterprise producing *inter alia* packaging, toys, office stationery, office machines) is a case of point. The Director of Personnel and Organization is quoted to the effect that 'Down to earth business is what counts here, not show. I could characterize the company by saying we are Rotterdam, rather than Amsterdam' (Mulder, 1989: 48).

A nice touch, this, especially as Buhrmann-Tetterode's head office is in Amsterdam, but Rotterdam in Dutch terms is the unpretentious, down-to-earth city where work gets done and money gets made.

Content Beheer, the employment bureau quoted earlier, occasionally encounters the status problem at one remove where, for example, a receiving organization to whom Content has hired an employee will not let the temp eat in the works canteen. Sales Manager Paulien van der Harst is appalled by such status-mongering:

You don't imagine that in such a case we are going to let our people take their food to work in a tupperware box. If there is tension between the role of Content as employer and the personnel arrangements of others [receiving organizations], then it is the importance of the people we are sending out that will weigh most heavily! (Mulder, 1989: 66)

The truck firm DAF knows where it stands on the status issue.

Says Personnel Director Ernst Godding: 'The company culture can be characterized in one word: no-nonsense. We have no truck with title-mongering. In the internal phone book for this company you won't find any academic titles in front of names' (Mulder, 1989: 72).

In the discussion of banking in Chapter 4 reference was made to the distinctive and eye-catching head office building of the NMB in Bijlmer, south Amsterdam. This building could be praised for its elegance and imagination, but the architect, Ton Alberts, embarked on a functional defence when interviewed by Mulder:

the building is actually much more functional than the hard, glass office boxes. They are too hot in the summer and too cold in the winter. We have placed functionality in the foreground, as much inside as outside. The slanting walls bounce back the noise from the motorway over the building so that nobody is bothered by it. (Mulder, 1989: 214)

Another theme is the corporate aversion to money spent on overheads, appearances, or luxury, Polynorm, which was cited earlier as a company whose work relations were affected by the strict Calvinism of Dutch society, is a case in point. On one occasion General Motors sent a delegation to Polynorm to vet them as suppliers, and the visit was later written up in the magazine *Auto.* ' "One thing we know for sure," said the astonished American to the company management, "there is absolutely no question of inflated overhead costs raising your prices" ' (Mulder, 1989: 239).

Polynorm's Managing Director Peter Huisman is quite happy with this American compliment, and observes: 'So we don't put our money into an expensive building that is going to serve as head office, but we will invest in the factory' (Mulder, 1989: 239). Mulder boldly comments that both Huisman and the other directors are often to be found on the shop floor.

Confectionery company van Melle has a similar dislike of luxury spending, as noted by Mulder: 'Members of the board and sales peoples get a company car. But obviously luxurious models are taboo. Izaak van Melle: "If people are looking for luxury they had better not come and work here" ' (Mulder, 1989: 269). Mulder notes that van Melle himself drives a BMW, but he bought it second hand. Underlying all these testimonies is a hint of the disapprobation you would incur if the norms were violated. Sometimes this rises to the surface, as in Mulder's account of FHV/BBDO, the Netherlands biggest advertising agency:

Even Jaques Kuyf (Account Manager) makes it clear that employees are not to get the idea that they should act glamorous, even though advertising has the reputation for being a world of glamour and glitter. However, self-mockery, and the ability to relativize/put things in context are valued more than expensive cars and fast talk. 'One of our people learned this when he turned up once in a big Mercedes, even though it wasn't a brand new car. A notice with Herr on it promptly appeared in his parking place. This is the way we cut people down to size.' (Mulder 1989: 97)

Part of the point of this story is that 'Mr' is spelled *Heer* in Dutch; only the Germans spell it *Herr*, as in the quoted excerpt. A nice touch, this: see off individual conceit and the memory of the Nazi invaders in one go. This account of the FHV/BBDO agency has a wider interest in that the desire to get away from the popular image of the advertising world is a leitmotiv. Personal modesty, long-term relationships with clients, and a stable company leadership are the things that are valued.

Common Sense in Dutch Business

Some of the issues raised in the last few pages—the antipathy to luxury and status-mongering, the rejection of personal conceit and corporate extravagance—will be seen as primarily negative, as condemnations of undesirable behaviour. Yet this state of mind gives rise in Dutch business life to an often estimable pragmatism. Take DAF as an example. Roger Gijzels, head of truck assembly, speaks glowingly to Mulder about the model choice offered by DAF, how well it compares with the narrower range offered by Ford and Mercedes, the competitive engagement of the production workers in meeting daily quotas. Gijzels ends with the homely exhortation 'Just go and sit in the pub. Then you'll hear how people talk about DAF' (Mulder, 1989: 71). It is a nice acolade, one that could cause redundancies in the PR industry. Ernst Godding, DAF's Personnel Director, told Mulder:

At DAF we are all a bit truck-crazy. Three quarters of the Board [*raad van bestuur*] have got a heavy goods licence. That includes Aart van der Padt, the Chairman. I have to get behind the wheel of a lorry at least a few times each year. I have driven our new 95 model in the Sierra Nevada in Spain. That's how you identify with the product. (Mulder, 1989: 74)

Is this not the ultimate in pragmatism: driving the trucks is worth a ton of management theory. The same need to keep your feet on the ground is to be seen at the exemplary Content Beheer, the employment bureau. Director Sylvia Toth concludes: 'I don't want as a matter of course to sit with my head in the clouds and just have contact with staff functions and management. I am conscious how much our company depends on its ordinary employees. Because they are the people who are going to express and realize our "corporate identity" in the outside world' (Mulder, 1989: 68).

DAF has its trucks, and Content Beheer its temps, and both have got reality into focus. The same philosophy is expressed by Henk Westerlaken, deputy chairman of the Board (*raad van bestuur*) of Center Parcs, who confided to Mulder that he made a point of staying in the parks, with his family, several times a year: 'That is something I find a must, in order to know how it is going, to check out the ethos, and not to lose contact with guests' (Mulder, 1989: 54).

In my own discussions with Dutch managers a similar strain towards the pragmatic has been consistently evident. They are much happier speaking of products and people, deeds and deals, than engaging in dicussions of management theory, or the principles behind the action. Ironically the Dutch are more like the Germans in this than the more self-consciously management-professional British and Americans.

A Dutch Informality

The Dutch not only tend towards informality of style and atmosphere, they recognize that companies will have an informal system side by side with the formal. By 'informal system' is meant the totality of contacts, networks, and practices alongside what is formally presented by the organization. The British and Americans tend to take it for granted that such an informal system will exist, that it is important, and that knowing how to work it belongs to managerial *savoir faire*. Interestingly, most of the classic studies of the informal system at work are American.

None of this should lead us to believe that the informal system is a universal phenomenon. It is clear, for example, from Michel Crozier's case studies in France that both the notion and the reality are quite attenuated there (Crozier, 1964). I have also argued elsewhere that companies in both Germany (Lawrence, 1980) and Sweden (Lawrence and Spybey, 1986) are much less likely to exhibit such informal systems. In Germany, for instance, what is formally ordained is much more likely to be what actually happens. Thus it is a significant—differentiating—fact that informal systems are widely recognized in the Netherlands.

The phenomenon is probably most readily observable in the big multinational companies. These are typically marked by a high degree of organizational complexity, and the ability of the Dutch to cope with this complexity has already been noted. In part this ability embraces the readiness to operate informal systems, which serve to buttress and sustain the formal. In particular individual managers in such companies will speak of having various informal networks, and these become layered as careers develop. Such networks may have a variety of bases in the larger companies: you will know, and probably always loosely keep in touch with, people who started their careers at the same time as yourself—loose networks of intake cohorts. Then as you move around the company you will have sequential groups of informally known people at different physical sites—the Zwolle group, the people at Hengelo, the Apeldoorn mob, and so on. And you will gradually extend the network of people with whom you share a function—design, quality control, purchasing, or whatever—but on a company-wide not site-specific basis. Successful careers in larger companies will also be punctuated with episodes of training, usually in the form of in-house courses. These again are fruitful ground for extending your range of contacts: people who share the challenge and opportunities of training courses often form a durable bond.

Again this phenomenon emerges clearly in the Mulder interviews, as attested, for example, by Unilever sales and marketing director Rob Polet:

There exists inside Unilever an awful lot of informal networks. And you really must not shut yourself off from these. In the ten years I have been with the company I have made masses of good friends during the courses and seminars that take place. That means colleagues with whom you maintain enduring contact during your career. If some time you have a problem, then you phone someone. Such personal contact can also play a role when you are looking for someone to fill a vacancy in your own organization. (Mulder, 1989: 262)

The same basic sentiment is echoed by a director of the publishing house Wolters Kluwer: 'I have my own network and via the informal channels I hear plenty and know all the time what is going on inside the organization. I often make the rounds and my door is open to everyone. The informal structure is at least as important as the formal' (Mulder, 1989: 300).

The connection between informal network and promotion is also made by Heineken employees in a company-administered survey: 'A large number of those asked worked on the assumption that in matters of promotion knowing the right person is important. In fact 30 per cent found that promotion is more determined by the people you know than by the performance you achieve' (Mulder 1989: 137).

Earlier in the chapter we demonstrated the Dutch aversion to pretension and status differences. It goes without saying that informality is viewed in a positive way. Consider again the redoubtable NMB bank profiled in the previous chapter. Hans Zwarts is their Personnel and Organization Director, and came to NMB from a 'turn-round' post at the troubled Vredesteen tyre company. He was probably expecting something more formal on joining a bank:

Within the shortest time everyone was using the intimate form of address.[1] The office doors of most of the managers stand open all the time, including mine. That informal character you find right up to the level of *raad van bestuur*. If you want to talk to a member of the *raad* you can be sure of getting him on the telephone. Naturally there is a bit of distance between the very top and the rest of the bank. That's true in a metaphorical as well as a literal sense, since in our new building [the attractive head office described in Chapter 4] the top people have their own wing. But on anniversary celebrations when there is sport, most of them are there. Two members of the *raad van bestuur*, Soetekouw and Van der Boor, were members of the eleven that played football against the team from the *ondernemingsraad* [works council]. (Mulder, 1989: 217)

Director and works council members playing football is quite something: even the Germans cannot claim that, and neither the British nor the Americans have a works council that could field a team.

The Importance of Being Dutch

The wording of this subheading is taken from an article by Dutch psychologist and management professor, Geert Hofstede (Hofstede, 1975). The gist of the article is that the Dutch give a greater weight to leisure, family, environment, and quality of life factors in evaluating the attractiveness of jobs, than do employees of some other nationalities.

This view has also been a theme of the present book to this point. Chapter 1 pointed to a Dutch business internationalism, based on adaptation not assertiveness. Chapter 2 sought to depict a balanced society, an amalgam of competing allegiances and structures, not the social stuff of which monomaniacs are made. In Chapter 3 we turned the spotlight for a moment on to employee demands brought to the CAO negotiations. Quite striking here from a British viewpoint was the lack of emphasis on monetary reward, but a corresponding concern for

- the unemployed
- training
- provision of apprenticeship places
- policy on youth employment
- equal opportunities for women
- remuneration of sick employees
- leisure time.

This is a distinctive list.

Again in Chapter 4 we paused for a moment to contrast the aspirations of British and Dutch employees in software houses in the Netherlands. The Dutch again were distinguished by an interest in

- training and personal development
- the intrinisic interest of the work
- the standing of the company's clients
- leisure time
- pension provision.

Another way to appraise the Dutch understanding of jobs is to see how they are advertised, and to seek comparisons with the USA and Britain. By far the best source here is the weekly paper *Intermediair*, a collection of economic and cultural features, followed by a substantial offering of management and administrative jobs. Scanning these for much of the 1980s a contrast with the usual Anglo-American presentation is indeed obvious.

If we approach the contrast first in a negative way, the typical Anglo-American emphasis on material reward is largely absent from the Dutch advertisements, at least until recently. There is not the same proclamation of salary, competitive earning, stock options, and fringe benefits. The typical Dutch advertisement does not mention salary at all or simply says that remuneration will be in line with the current CAO: in Dutch companies the CAO agreements covering wages and salaries often go a long way up the hierarchy, covering a lot of staff and management people. Fringe benefits do not usually figure at all.

Looked at positively, there are also differences. The emphasis is on the intrinsic interest of the work, training and development, job security, and the work atmosphere. The latter is typically praised in terms of decency, friendliness, and informality, and team spirit certainly figures.

But perhaps the last word should be left with Heineken, and the results of one of their in-house surveys, which is discussed by Henk Mulder. With regard to which aspects of the job people saw as most desirable, the following proportions emerged:

Pleasure in the work	60%
Decent remuneration	47%
Interesting work	46%
Ability to take decisions	41%
Likeable colleagues	40%
Feeling valued as a person	37%

It is also noted that 'working for a successful company' and 'job security' scored high with Heineken employees, though no percentages are given (Mulder, 1989: 136–7). From an Anglo-American viewpoint this is indeed another country.

Note

[1] Dutch, like French and German, has two words for you, a formal and an informal version. In the Dutch original Zwarts speaks of everyone addressing each as other as *je* and *jij* instead of using the more formal *U*.

6

Style and Disposition

HONESTY, a touch of Calvinist rectitude, a tendency to conformity, a respect for facts and a favouring of verifiability, a hostility to luxury and extravagance, a dislike of status-mongering and liking for informality, and a conviction that common sense is a guiding principle in management—these are some ingredients of a Dutch management style canvassed in the previous chapter, where I also attempted to trace their derivation in terms of Dutch society and values. The purpose here is to continue that exercise, but focusing more on what Dutch management is like rather than on the social origins of such characteristics of style.

The Flamboyant Dutchman?

Dutch management is seldom flamboyant or swashbuckling in style. The Dutch business scene seems little inclined to throw up striking personalities of the John Harvey Jones or Lee Iacoca kind, and the Dutch general public makes less of them (and until the 1980s made nothing of them at all).

In British and American writing about management, and particularly in recruitment advertisements, the idea that the good manager is dynamic, proactive, assertive, and self-consciously aware of his or her power-propensity is a recurring theme. This ethic is not absent in Dutch management, but it is much more muted (and again until the 1980s was rare indeed). The point urged here is not that Dutch management is undynamic, but that the cult of personal dynamism is largely absent. Dynamism, proactivity, and assertion are not the colours under which Dutch management sails.

Consider simply how inappropriate some of the American shiboleths sound. Where is Dutch management's 'killer instinct', their 'hire and fire' mentality? Where in the Netherlands is Michael Maccoby's 'gamesman' as a management type, never mind the 'jungle fighter' (Maccoby, 1978). There is a related idea of business and management as a tough, high-pressure world, whose surviving denizens will need the constitution of an ox and the *esprit* of the battlefield commander. An American chief executive I interviewed recently claimed with irrepressible delight: 'It is hot in this kitchen—and not everyone can stand the heat!' Dutch chief executives do not say things like this. Dutch management is not self-consciously macho.

A contrast can also be made between Dutch and French management styles. French management is distinguished above all else by a formal, educated cleverness. Most French managers are recruited from the *grandes écoles*, a group of 'super-universities' practising a highly competitive, differential recruitment and sustaining an expressly élitist culture (Barsoux and Lawrence, 1990). Furthermore, these antecedents inform French management deportment and behaviour. In a society which has always esteemed the intellectual, the philosopher, and the serious writer, the French manager is an exponent of *culture générale*, never at a loss at a dinner party or cocktail reception, ever ready to engage in wider conversation and to discuss non-business themes. French managers at work display their educated strengths. They parade their powers of analysis and synthesis, they exhibit a ready mastery of the complicated, they can formulate arguments (and spot the *non sequitur* in arguments formulated by others). At a more tangible level the typical French manager is a good prose stylist, likes written communication, and enjoys formal meetings—as an arena in which to deploy educated cleverness. French managers even on occasion correct the prose of their subordinates, feel a duty to instruct them in the mysteries of the French subjunctive—the true meaning of *noblesse oblige* (Barsoux and Lawrence, 1990).

Dutch management is patently not like this. As was suggested in the discussion of the Dutch education system in Chapter 2, while Dutch managers are decently and relevantly qualified (a point which will be elaborated in the next chapter) they are not conspicuous for their educated cleverness. In the Netherlands the management process is not defined in ratiocinative terms, hierarchy and advancement are not legitimated by appeal to the lustre of formal qualifications—remember the DAF director's comment cited in Chapter 5 that their internal phone book contains no academic titles. This contrast between French and Dutch management is nicely brought out by the one educational achievement in which the Dutch are manifestly ahead of the French, namely foreign language—and especially English—speaking ability. Again, this feature of Dutch management will be taken up in a subsequent chapter; suffice it to say here that this ability is very widespread in the Netherlands. Now the interesting thing for the present comparison is how lightly the Dutch take their ability in this area. They do not make intellectual capital out of it. A Dutchman is always unassuming: the flair for languages is explained away with the (totally unconvincing) 'we are a small country' argument.

If the American style is one of macho dynamism, and if the French strength is educated cleverness, what of German management? Does this again offer a contrast with the Dutch? There is a fairly widespread belief that the Germans are authoritarian, that they like giving and receiving orders, have a *Befehl ist Befehl* ('orders are orders') mentality, and a touch of ruthlessness. It is not difficult to see how this has arisen, given the history of Germany in general and the period of the Third Reich and the Second World War in particular. This general attribution of authoritarianism also furnishes a foreign characterization of German management as authority-driven and terrible in its power to exact compliance. This is the view that finds expression in British jokes along the lines of 'when the German foreman says jump, the reply is, how high boss?'

Now it can be argued that this characterization of German management is both misleading and unjustified, that German industry in the post-war period has been proud of its egalitarian and classless ethos, that German managers use their rank and titles much less than foreigners think they do, that Germany like the Netherlands, indeed some twenty years before, has established a system of industrial democracy. Or again that German managers are more critical of their seniors than are their English counterparts

(Hutton and Lawrence, 1979): the German foreman is at his most menacing telling management 'where to get off'. German managers, if questioned about their style, will often refer to an open-door policy, talk about seeing it for yourself (not taking it on trust from a higher authority), and espouse a critical climate often designated as 'constructive opposition' (Lawrence, 1980).

Yet despite all these counter-arguments there is something in the personal deportment of the German manager that lends verisimilitude to the popular stereotype. The German manager is often marked by a certain resoluteness. German managers do not look restrained, subtle, and tolerant; they appear resolute and decisive. The mien somehow suggests that German managers know where they are going and what they want, that everyone concerned will appreciate the rightness of their intentions, and that what they intend is going to happen.

The point here is that while Dutch management style may resemble the German in some matters of formal democracy and informal equality, the Dutch manager does not parade decisiveness, is not self-consciously resolute, has a more restrained and conditional 'world view'.

The Handy Dutchman

So far we have sought to say something about Dutch management style reactively, by denoting other national styles and comparing the Dutch style to these. But the subject can also be approached positively. In the Dutch mind there is something of a Dutch management style which goes beyond the informal–unpretentious–common-sense syndrome elaborated in the last chapter. The Dutch sometimes express this idea by saying that the good Dutch manager is *handig*.

If you look up *handig* in the dictionary it gives it as 'clever' or 'handy', but in the context of the successful manager it means a little more—able to convince and persuade, 'sell' things to people, get agreement, do deals, bring people together. As one respondent put it: 'There is well-trained explicit behaviour in attaining your own targets. One is always in a bargaining situation. The successful manager is always a good bargainer. A sound integrator. We say, *hij is handig*, he makes good manœuvres, not Machiavellian, not just social integration, and certainly not just task-orientated, but *handig!'*

This captures some of what is in the Dutch mind. Dutch style is not to be depicted in broad brush-strokes, it is a more subtle and conditional phenomenon. It is about bargaining without bludgeoning, persuasion not dynamism, manœuvring without menace, getting things done with a lightness of touch rather than the heavy hand of goal-driven decisiveness.

Outward Bound

Perhaps the essence of the Dutch formula is the exercise of initiative within constraints. Part of this initiative is the much-vaunted internationalism of Dutch business, the 'thinking beyond the borders', the readiness to go abroad and do things abroad, the drive to export. It is a phenomenon we sought to illustrate in Chapter 1, using Heineken as an example.

A variation on this theme is the Dutch ability to adapt abroad. It is not just a matter of linguistic talent, important though this is, but of humility and restraint. The Dutch abroad do not proclaim their nationality; Dutch companies abroad are not obviously and insistently Dutch, in the way that American companies are invariably consciously and distinguishably American. The same disposition seems to have underpinned the Dutch performance as a colonizing power. If you make the obvious comparison between the Dutch and the British as colonizers in the Far East, then the Dutch were more low profile, more matter-of-fact. They were less of a legend than the British, but they alienated fewer people. Their style was less remarkable but more acceptable. Their colonial enterprise was utility-driven, not inspired by the need to spread the Dutch way of life abroad. It is a contrast captured by one interviewee who remarked: 'In India everything is British, yet in Indonesia nothing is Dutch.'

The spawning and sustenance of a range of multinational companies described in Chapter 4 is another manifestation of this
initiative. The Dutch may be restrained, but they can and do
build large and complicated enterprises. What is more there are
too many of these 'large and complicated enterprises' in the
Netherlands for it to be anything but indicative. Consider that
the Dutch score in this matter includes one of the world's largest
oil companies, two chemical multinationals, one of the world's
top electronics firms, Europe's largest brewery, and the world's
oldest airline.

A further manifestation of this initiative is the phenomenon, in
part explored in Chapter 4, of the range of business and organizational types. In this connection we have already noted the
agricultural co-operatives, a heterogeneity of banking institutions,
the self-conscious organizational complexity of the multinationals,
the range of service organizations from employment bureau to
consultancy firms, from Center Parc to BSO (the cell-based software
house). This range of business enterprise and heterogeneity of
organizational form has not 'just happened'; it is a testimony to
the Dutch spirit of adventure.

Genius is Knowing Where to Stop

In his illuminating treatment of Bismarck, the architect of German
unification, the English historian A. J. P. Taylor applies a quotation
from Goethe, *'in der Beschränkung zeigt sich erst der Meister'*, colloquially rendered as 'genius is knowing where to stop' (Taylor,
1955). The essence of Taylor's judgement is that Bismarck succeeded by limiting his objectives, by not espousing ambitions of
world domination, by underplaying his hand. Perhaps a less happy
rendering of the line from Goethe would be 'mastery shows itself
in a recognition of limitations'. It provides apt testimony to that
Dutch strength of the initiative that recognizes constraints. But
what in this connection are the constraints?

There are essentially three views of time. The first is that it does
not matter, a view that appears to Western businessmen to be

espoused by much of the Third World. The second view is that it does matter, but with effort and resource man can impose his will on it, stretch it, manipulate it, and outwit it as needs arise—Israeli managers are the *par excellence* exponents of this view (Lawrence, 1990). The third view, dominant in the Western world, is that time is an objective reality that confronts man in his intentions and doings. As exemplars of the last view the Dutch are rivalled only by the Germans.

The most obvious manifestation of this view is that Dutch managers engage in realistic operational planning: they do not expect time to 'stand up and beg' to accommodate their plans, they expect to accommodate to it. Again, the Dutch are diligent in the matter of appointments, in recording them and keeping them. Time for them is part of man's contract with reality.

There is also an industrial as well as a managerial manifestation of this disposition. In Britain, from the mid-1970s onwards, a series of studies was carried out on delivery performance, the degree to which consignments of goods are delivered to customers by manufacturers on time (Lawrence, 1984). These British studies on the whole give cause for concern, and the one internationally comparative study puts Britain in last place (that is, worst delivery performance) out of five European countries (Turnbull and Cunningham, 1981). What of the Dutch?

The engaging thing is that there appear to be no comparable studies of delivery performance in the Netherlands, nor does the Netherlands figure in the international study cited above. It would seem that delivery performance is simply not an issue, not because it does not matter, but because there are no 'commissions of inquiry' into things that are going well. At the level of managerial behaviour the respect for time shades into a strong desire to be, and to be seen as, reliable. It was suggested in Chapter 2 that reliability is perceived as a regional variable in the Netherlands, with the north believing itself to be 'better at it' than the south. Whether or not this regional comparison is valid, the interesting thing is that reliability is seen as being important enough to be worth making the comparison.

In the same way that the Dutch feel themselves to be confronted by the objectivity of time, they have a respect for all that comprises both the human and the natural environment.

Being reliable is part of that respect. The human environment means other people's needs, expectations, and wishes. Meeting the reasonable expectations of others, satisfying their needs where possible, predictably doing your bit within a mosaic of co-operation, in short being reliable, is thus a natural and reasonable response to the human condition.

It is sometimes suggested that the Dutch penchant for punc-tuality and reliability derives from the respect the Dutch have to accord to the natural environment. Because much of the Nether-lands is below sea level, and some of it is reclaimed land, sea protection with an elaborate system of dams and dykes is critical. As a Dutch accountant put it to me: 'If we get this wrong we get our feet wet.' As with nature, so with man.

The concern with facts and details is no doubt part of the same phenomenon. While linked to a humble conception of self rather than to vaunting egotism, as suggested in Chapter 5, taking the facts seriously, mastering the details, is again part of taking the environment seriously. You do not expect to impose your will on this environment as a simple consequence of being. The Dutch do not share the instinctive American belief that everything is possible, that man can do anything, that it is just a matter of organization and resources. The Dutch view is more constrained and conditioned: it may be possible; you have to consider, master the facts, check it over, figure out which levers to pull and tilt.

Business Morality

In a fascinating inaugural lecture at the University of Limburg in the southern town of Maastricht, Geert Hofstede suggested that the Netherlands can be understood in terms of some representative social types (Hofstede, 1987). One of these is the preacher. The Dutch, he suggested, quite like the idea that they know what is right for other people, and have a duty to tell them (preach). It is the one piece of Dutch exuberance. This is relfected in the Dutch engagement in international affairs. The Dutch are well informed about the rest of the world. Because of their colonial history they have a particular interest in Indonesia, South Africa, and parts of the West Indies. Somewhat later their experiences in the Second World War helped to make them staunch Europeans, co-operators with other European countries. They had a customs union with Belgium and Luxembourg before the inception of the Common Market, and were founder members of the latter in 1957–8. They were keen to see the EC enlarged, especially by the entry of Britain (and have been disappointed by Britain's lack of European spirit ever since). The Dutch also feel their ideals and commitment confer the right to judge.

It is usually assumed that this is part of the Calvinist legacy, that Calvinism, with its ethic of personal responsibility, supplies both the ideals and a touch of rectitude. It may be, however, that there is another dimension, that the Dutch response to the environment embraces a respect for its moral dynamics, that the Dutch have a natural appreciation of the need for ethical regulation, parallel to their appreciation of the need to regulate the physical environment (Shetter, 1987).

All this has a variety of implications for business and management behaviour. First, there is the Dutch hostility to bribery mentioned earlier. A strong line on bribery is particularly remarkable for a country with a colonial past and extensive overseas operations in the present. It is also significant that Dutch managers with overseas experience pick out aversion to bribery as a defining characteristic of Dutch business behaviour. It is also interesting that bribery and corruption are among the sins for which the Dutch most enjoy condemning others.

Second, there is the related issue of Dutch respect for the law. Dutch companies tend to be naturally law-abiding, and not necessarily for fear of being caught out. The American idea that the corporation's sole commitment is to profit, and that a company may well break the law in pursuit of its profit objectives and simply rely on 'heavy-duty' litigation to get it off the hook after the event, is quite foreign to the Netherlands.

Third, there is the matter of the Dutch contribution to Third

World aid. The Dutch are ready contributors and their contribution is generous. There are also moral–psychological rewards in line with the preacher image. Not only can you condemn countries that have more but give less; the Dutch business establishment can happily rail against countries engaged in tied aid. Aid is said to be tied when the receiving countries can only spend the money on goods and services produced by the donor country. France is the example that the Dutch like to cite (and condemn). In fact a recent account of aid in Africa suggests that Dutch virtue here is not quite as pristine as they like to think. The idea is that while the Netherlands does not tie aid in the hard sense noted above, it may be tied *de facto* by being linked to projects in relation to which the Netherlands has a competitive advantage—as advisor, contractor, or supplier.

Fourth, there is the wider issue of business morality, going beyond the particular instance of bribery. Although this judgement is not to be treated as absolute, it is generally the case that the conduct of business and management in the Netherlands is more rather than less moral than that of the Anglo-Saxon world. The idea of institutionalized cheating is less prevalent in the Netherlands than in, say, Britain. There is less acceptance of the notion that for either business gain or personal career advantage you may sail close to the wind, do things that are not really allowed or acceptable, and that if you can get away with it people will have a sneaking regard for you.

One possible manifestation of this is that there does not appear to be an ostensibly witty yet semi-serious literature on career or business success in the Netherlands. The Dutch appear to be neither producers nor consumers of the 'how to hack, stab, and intrigue your way to the top' genre of writing. Although this literature is intended largely to entertain and could not actually be used as a practical guide, it does reflect an Anglo-American view that business and career needs may subordinate conventional morality.

A possibility related point is that in the Netherlands there is probably less in the way of minor acts of manipulation in the process of supervision and control. In Britain and America the tendency is for supervisors and managers to like to have some-thing—and not always an official something—with which to reward compliance or sanction deviance among subordinates. Now this does go on to some extent in the Netherlands, but it appears to figure less and does not come up as a minor source of satisfaction when people give accounts of their jobs and how they get things done. There are probably two reasons for this.

The first, already canvassed in the earlier discussion of industrial democracy and collective bargaining (see Chapter 3), is that Dutch culture is more explicit and contractual about what is required and allowed. So it is that much more difficult for Dutch managers to preserve an area of discretion in matters of reward or sanction: either employees are allowed something, or they are not, and it will be written down somewhere.

The second reason is that this kind of control resource seems to be less necessary in that employees are more self-disciplined. Such discipline will not show in acts of deference, restrained deportment, formal clothing, or a submissive demeanour, but in actual work behaviour. This is not to say that Dutch workers are overly docile, but rather that they pursue their legitimate aspirations (or fractious demands, depending on your point of view) through trade union support, collective bargaining, and works council representation. Dutch workplace behaviour appears disciplined in the sense that employees are less likely to engage in acts of minor disruption, to use shortcomings in management, or the organization of work, as an excuse to down tools; they are more likely to feel it is their duty to do the best job they can with the tools and materials to hand, even if these are not perfect.

If you question Dutch production managers about ongoing problems or constraints on output they tend to mention technical factors or matters relating to 'inbound logistics' (Johnson and Scoles, 1989). There are virtually no references in this context to the range of minor industrial relations issues—complaints about working conditions, work allocation, overtime, subcontracting, supervision, recognition, demarcation, and so on—that used to be the 'daily round' of life in British manufacturing (Lawrence, 1984).

Style and Disposition

Careerism and the Dutch Spirit

Careerism appears to be less pronounced among Dutch managers than among their Anglo-American colleagues, and in so far as career striving is encouraged and made explicit it is largely a phenomenon of the 1980s.

In Britain and the USA it is thought quite normal for managers to be ambitious. It is expected that they will seek advancement, together with increases in power and remuneration. They may not all in fact do this, but it is normal to have such aspirations and people may be frank about them. Furthermore, management rhetoric assumes a near-universal desire for promotion and advancement, an exhortatory literature purports to tell people how to be successful (do a good job and get promoted), and recruitment practices and especially job advertisements are heavily suffused with appeals to the drive and achievement that deserves reward.

All this is much less pronounced in the Netherlands; as already mentioned, a modicum of explicit careerism really only became acceptable in the 1980s. It is interesting to consider the reasons for this constraint.

First, as suggested in Chapter 5 where some of Hofstede's findings were discussed, non-work factors seem more important to the Dutch. Here the reference is to the rival claims of family, leisure, community, environment, and other interests (Hofstede, 1975). It is suggested here that the Dutch really are different from the British or Americans in this respect, Hofstede would seem to support this view, but at the same time the mythological difference is important. Whatever American managers actually think and feel, the expectation that they will put work first, make sacrifices for it, and see career advance as a life plan, is very much stronger than in the Netherlands.

Second—and again the idea has been introduced previously at several points—in the world of work itself the promotion–power–remuneration syndrome is not necessarily viewed as the most important aspect of work. Again rival claims of work environment, agreeable colleagues, friendly atmosphere, and intrinsic work interest may and often do take precedence. Job security and pension rights also seem to be more highly valued than in Britain or America, while training is seen more in terms of personal development rather than career advancement (consider in this connection the Heineken survey quoted in Chapter 5, and the discussion of the work aspirations of software specialists in Chapter 4).

Third, the promotion ethic founders somewhat on Dutch constraints on individuality and personal pride. To strive for advancement is to claim something that most people will not get. To suggest a higher degree of personal merit, to push yourself forward and claim to be different—all these are things that the Dutch do not like.

Any reader who is not convinced by these claims is invited to look at advertisements for management posts in British newspapers. The biggest lettering is reserved for the salary, centrally positioned in the advert space. The salary is supported by a further package of material inducements—car, BUPA, relocation allowance, expenses, and so on. The typical advert is strong on appeals to, and recognition of, promotional dynamism. By these standards Dutch management advertisements are matter-of-fact, low-profile, non-materialistic, and unaggressive—and if you go back only to the mid-1980s the contrast is more marked.

Strategy and Common Sense

Corporate strategy, like so much else in the business world, is an American invention. But during the 1980s this notion swept the industrialized world and the Netherlands is no exception. The essence of strategy is that companies will have a vision of the future, make decisions about the scope and nature of their business, set objectives, formulate plans for their realization, allocate resources appropriately, and monitor and control performance in line with strategic plans. All this is quite acceptable in the Netherlands, indeed corporate strategy is now rather fashionable. But if you take the USA as the base-line there are one or two variations in the Dutch case.

One of these is that the strategic enterprise is viewed less uncritically than in its homeland. For the Dutch, strategy may be a means to an end, but it is not the holy grail. There are elements of Dutch scepticism, and you will, for example, be told of the possible dysfunctions of target-setting. This covers such instances as unit managers holding down results in year one so as to show a gain in year two, or maximizing against the business plan (to make sure they reach or surpass targets) in the short term in the expectation of moving on (being promoted) so they do not have to live with the consequences.

A second point of interest is that in American orthodoxy strategy is proclaimed. Strategic analysis and choice may be the prerogative of those at the top, but when it is in place it should be explicit. Indeed, strategic objectives should be cascaded down through the organization, raising employee consciousness and informing behaviour at all levels. The Dutch do not do this. It is not exactly that they are secretive, but they would find the 'strategy cascade' slightly distasteful. It would be an invasion of employee privacy, where motivation is a personal attribute.

There is a wider phenomenon here. Dutch managers take work and company objectives seriously, but sometimes react against the intense professionalism of the Americans. The serious American focus on the minutiae of marketing and strategy, performance monitoring and accountability, sometimes seems a little excessive to the Dutch.

7

The Character of Dutch Management

IN the two foregoing chapters we have explored the style and inclinations of Dutch managers, linking some of their dispositions to Dutch values. In the present chapter I would like to add another dimension to the understanding of Dutch management by considering a range of its characteristics, for the most part dealing in that which may be observed rather than, as previously, in that which may be inferred.

Education

In a straightforward and formal sense Dutch management is well educated. In this the country is clearly on a level with most of continental Europe, and the education level of executives in the Netherlands would probably be exceeded only by that in France, where managers are very largely recruited from the *grandes écoles*. There are probably proportionally fewer managers in the Netherlands with a doctorate than is the case in neighbouring West Germany, but the Dutch doctorate is more difficult to obtain—at least the standard time for acquiring a doctorate is as a full-time student ('assistant in training' is the modern expression) is longer in the Netherlands than in Germany. The education level of Dutch management compares favourably with that in Britain. The proportion of graduate managers is probably higher in the Netherlands, though there are insufficient data for a precise comparison. But the most noticeable difference is the relative absence in Dutch management of people with a minimum school leaving certificate who have worked their way up from blue-collar, junior technical, or clerical work—which is common in Britain.

The second point to be made about the educational background of Dutch managers is that there is a strong patterning as to subjects studied, the three traditional subjects for people entering commercial or industrial management being law, economics, and engineering. This triad of subjects might well be described as typical of continental Europe (excepting France where the subject choice is less clear-cut and the comparison made more difficult by a two-tier higher education system). In addition to this traditional triad the 1980s have seen the rise of management itself as a university subject, and a vast increase in its popularity. Indicative of this trend is the fact that the Nijenrode management college discussed in Chapter 2 achieved university status in the late 1980s.

There does not seem to be a literature in the Netherlands devoted to a discussion of the rival merits of the various subjects in terms of career progression and making it to the top, though there are studies bearing on this theme in, for instance, both Britain and West Germany. There is, however, some folk wisdom as to which institutions are to be regarded as the cradles of executive greatness. The Leiden University law school is often mentioned in this connection, and so to a lesser extent is the Utrecht law school. If these are the traditional starting points for successful careers in Dutch business, the currently fashionable launching pad is to do *bedrijfseconomie* (business economics) at Erasmus University in Rotterdam.

Finally on the education front it should be underlined that the Dutch system has two tiers, that the second level of qualification below that of the university degree, the HBO level described in Chapter 2, is important in the Dutch scheme of things. This does not go without saying. There are some countries where this second, sub-university degree level has never been very important—France is an example. There are others, including Britain, where the second level, as represented by the old Higher National Certificate qualification, has declined in importance in the face of an 'all graduate' ethos. But in the Netherlands the HBO qualification and courses are booming. Just about everyone in middle management and higher has either a university or HBO level education.

The Gift of Tongues

English-speaking ability in the Netherlands is very widespread, and it can be pretty well taken for granted that a Dutch manager will speak English. There are, perhaps, two additional points to be made. The first is that English is not only widely spoken in the Netherlands, but thoroughly domiciled there too. Knowing some English is just a natural part of being Dutch, for the majority of people. Dutch television, for example, shows many English and American programmes, as does German television. But whereas German television dubs all these programmes in German, Dutch TV transmits them in English with rather cursory Dutch subtitles. Perhaps even more telling, on Dutch news and current affairs programmes, where there are interviews with newsworthy people, these are usually done in English (and also in German and some-times French) without a voice-over in Dutch, the expedient adopted in other countries. The same is true for interviews with British and American entertainers on the numerous pop music programmes.

The second point is that the Dutch language skill is not confined to English. German is widely spoken, and the ability to understand spoken German is near universal. The ability to speak some French is also by no means uncommon. In the MAVO secondary schools described in Chapter 2, which are like secondary modern schools in England before the comprehensive movement, all pupils learn French, German, and English as a matter of course. In short, the Dutch are not just good at English but good at languages. This gives them a considerable business advantage. It sustains the inter-nationalism symbolized by the example of Heineken in Chapter 1.

Techniek

In the 1980s the German word *Technik* became a household expression in Britain, largely through the series of Audi car advertisements ending with the punch-line *Vorsprung durch Technik*, suggesting competitive advantage through superior engineering. At another level, writing about Germany has tended to highlight the strength of German engineering, and the Germans' general technical orientation. Dutch, unlike English, has the equivalent word, *Techniek*, albeit with an additional vowel. This prompts the question, is this same general technical orientation observable in the Netherlands?

Now one answer to this question has already been canvassed in Chapter 4, where it was suggested that the Dutch economy tends to be 'light' on traditional manufacturing and strong in a variety of service and energy branches of industry. Indeed, as the table below suggests, traditional manufacturing industry has never

The structure of employment in the Netherlands (%)

	Agriculture	Industry	Services
1870	37	29	34
1960	11	41	48
1984	5	28	67

Source: Elfring, 1989: 338.

had the same importance as in Britain, Germany, or the USA, or as in such smaller comparable countries as Belgium and Sweden.

Despite this qualification as regards the relative importance of the different sectors of the economy, it is still possible to pursue the question of the presence or absence of a technical orientation.

In so far as the German strength has been counterposed to a British weakness, it might be argued that the Netherlands has more in common with Germany. The case may be argued in terms of an Anglo-Dutch contrast. First, there is no suggestion in the

Netherlands that either engineers or engineering lack status in industry or society. Second, the technical functions in Dutch companies—research and development, design, production control, production, engineering, maintenance, quality control—do not seem to lack status compared with the non-technical or commercial functions, nor to be perceived by Dutch managers as a second best career–promotion route. Indeed, there are in the Netherlands some strongly research-driven companies; Océ is one that has already been mentioned, and Philips is another, with its above average spending on research for that branch of industry. In short, while the Dutch economy is not as strongly oriented to manufacture as that of, say, Germany or Sweden, it does not appear to exhibit any of the anti-industrial snobberies that have been so much bemoaned in Britain since international comparisons became popular in the late 1970s.

At the same time the Dutch themselves tend to stress their commercial orientation. They are conscious of being an eary trading nation, and a former colonial power (in the Dutch litany of mid-twentieth-century misfortunes the loss of Indonesia, as it became, after the Second world War, ranks only after the defeat of 1940 and the German occupation itself). Today it is noticeable how many Dutch people speak of Indonesia with warmth and affection. Among older people who have lived there it comes across as a nostalgia for the country (whereas the British equivalent tends to be a nostalgia for a way of life).

The Dutch clearly like the idea of themselves as traders, and Dutch managers invariably emphasize their outward-looking orientation and the importance of exporting, even if their own jobs in the company have nothing to do with sales or exports. The Dutch similarly like the idea of themselves as adventurous traders—early, fearless, and imaginative seekers of commercial gain beyond the borders. As a Dutch business consultant put it to me at the end of 1989 with the opening up of East Germany: 'The Germans [that is, West Germans] will be their looking for investment opportunities, the Dutch to see what they can buy and sell!'

Generalism versus Specialism

It is possible to characterize management as having a generalist or specialist orientation. American orthodoxy favours generalism. The view is that there are general principles of management which have validity across a range of operations and branches of industry. At the core of the American notion of professional management is the action paradigm which stresses setting objectives, devising plans, allocating resources, implementing, and controlling, and this paradigm, of course, has a general applicability—it expresses the essence of what it is to manage a business.

Generalism has implications for management behaviour and careers. It goes hand in hand with a conscious professionalism; it facilitates an 'arms-length' approach while not inevitably requiring it; it leads to 'management by exception' (focusing on deviations from a plan and taking action on them), and enhances the standing of forecasting, planning, marketing, and control activities. It encourages, or at least legitimizes, a mobility between both functions and companies in personal careers, and stresses the importance of the overall view at the top.

A specialist view, however, tends to emphasize the specifics of company operation: what products are made? what markets are served? Specialism also enhances the integrity of particular functions (functions in the sense of design, production, sales, personnel, finance, and so on). The functions recruit on the basis of specialist knowledge and experience; careers are made within functions; inter-company mobility will only occur between companies in the same industry. Even the organizational format may be affected, with companies being agglomerations of functions, co-ordinated by a 'thin layer' of general management at the top.

Germany has traditionally exemplified this specialist approach, with an emphasis on specific knowledge and skills, especially technical ones—German industry tends to be design and production led. German managers as individuals will often identify themselves in specialist terms as, for instance, an export salesman, a production controller, a design engineer, a research chemist, and so on, rather than using the general label of manager.

So this is the generalist–specialist continuum, with the USA and Germany as polar types at either end of it. What of the Netherlands? In fact it is difficult to place the Netherlands in any unambiguous way. In the pattern of university subjects from which management is recruited, in the relative recency of management as a university subject and the scarcity of indigenous MBAs, the Netherlands has everything in common with Germany and little with the USA. The same finding holds even more strongly at the second level of HBO qualification, where courses are more explicitly vocational, with more specialisms on offer—some of these being specific to a branch of industry or type of work.

The same specialist leaning is to be seen in the way new (qualified) recruits to companies are treated. The expectation is that they will go into a particular function, learn it in practice and show their abilities in it, and certainly stay with it for the first few years. The 'cooks tour' traineeship or rapid succession of assignments common in the Britain and the USA appears to be less favoured in the Netherlands. Furthermore, mobility between companies and employers has, until the late 1980s, been strongly discouraged (the theme of manager mobility will be discussed in more detail a little later). This traditional disapproval of mobility is quite important for the assessment of generalism–specialism, since personnel mobility between companies is a major means of developing the generalist reputation.

But this is not the whole story. If you ask Dutch personnel managers engaged in recruitment what they look for, you get a mix of generalist and specialist factors. Certainly the latter do not predominate, even for technical jobs, in the way that they do in the accounts given by German personnel managers. In the Dutch case personal qualities, communication skills, and variations on the theme of being *handig* (explained in Chapter 6) all figure. This impression is substantiated by analysing the forms, checklists, and scoring sheets used by personnel interviewers in Dutch companies.

Another manifestation of this qualified Dutch generalism is the apparent over-representation of lawyers in senior positions. Of the Continental trio of traditional subjects for managers to have studied—law, economics, and engineering—law is the most general, lacking the functional application of the other two. Law is regarded as a training for management precisely because it will develop certain general qualities—the power of analysis and formulation, the ability to sift and weigh evidence, the power of advocacy. This argument about the role of law, it has to be admitted, is not an unqualified contribution to the case for Dutch generalism, in that genuine generalist considerations overlap with traditional status ones, symbolized by the role of Leiden law school as an Ivy League institution.

The final argument about Dutch management generalism is more an impression than anything else. In interviews with Dutch managers, especially senior managers, the generalist virtues are apparent. They are not overlaid with the fierce professionalism of American management, it is of a more proven, matter-of-fact, and homely kind, but it is perceptible.

Relations between Departments

Any business enterprise that progresses beyond a minimal size will cease to be a 'seamless garment' organizationally speaking and will be increasingly differentiated into departments or functions. So a typical manufacturing company will have the functions of design, purchasing, production (with a 'supporting cast' of related sub-functions—production control, production engineering, main-tenance, quality control, packing and dispatch), sales and/or marketing, personnel, finance, and perhaps legal affairs and public relations.

It is only a short step from this differentiation of companies into functions and departments to a situation where the people staffing each of these functions think of themselves as particularly valuable to the company. It is easy to see how this occurs. People are recruited to particular functions on the basis of special skills and relevant experience, or at least a presumed aptitude for the work in question. They are socialized in the importance of this work; their 'definition of reality' is reinforced by those people with whom they have most contact—colleagues in the same function. The function's contribution to the whole becomes an end in itself; empire-building is not only understandable but a professional duty.

We have parodied the phenomenon a little, but it is both a reality and a widespread one, attested in various British and American studies (Dalton, 1959; Lawrence, 1984). The question here is how poignant are such issues in companies in the Netherlands?

A first point of interest concerns the extent to which the functions are differentiated by status. In Britain there is both survey and salary data evidence to suggest that the functions are informally perceived as constituting a rough status hierarchy, in which finance and marketing are high-status functions, while design, engineering, and production are low in status (Lockyer and Jones, 1980; Hutton and Lawrence, 1982). The interesting thing is that there seems to be little of this in the Netherlands.

On several occasions I have tried to probe this phenomenon with open-ended questions both to Dutch managers employed in several of these functions and to general managers and consultants 'above the fray'. Such open-ended probing does not usually produce any reaction. There are also some comparative salary data which appear to support the view that there is little status differentiation between the functions, in so far as you would expect status differences to go hand in hand with salary differences, as is the case in Britain. The study concerned, by Anton Buys, takes the salary of the managing director (MD) as 100, and expresses the salaries of functional directors—sales, production, personnel, and so on—in relation to this 100 in each of five countries including the Netherlands (Buys, 1985).

In broad terms Buys's study shows a narrower salary spread, implying less differentiation, in the Netherlands, than in Belgium, West Germany, France, or Switzerland. To take a few particular cases the salary gap between the MD and their deputy or division head is smaller in the Netherlands than in the other countries; so is the salary gap between the MD and the sales director, production director, works director, administration director, and finance director; and the relative salary disadvantage of the research and development director compared with the MD is smaller in the Netherlands than in the other countries in the study except France,

France being well known for rewarding high formal qualifications amongst managers (Sylvester, 1971). Finally, the automation director is better paid relative to the MD in the Netherlands than in the other countries including, surprisingly, West Germany.

In short there is evidence, both 'hard' and 'soft' of a sort of function, salary, and status compression. This is interesting in itself, and it is an obvious manifestation of the Dutch egalitarianism discussed earlier. It may also be significant for understanding relations between the various functions.

This brings us to the second point of interest, and, again taking Britain as a reference point, it seems not only that differences in status and promotion prospects between the various functions are at least informally acknowledged, but that relationships between the functions are often critical and have recourse to hostile stereotypes (Lockyer and Jones, 1980). This thesis has been worked out in some detail for the production function in Britain (Hutton and Lawrence, 1982). The production function, it should be said, is a strategic site for studying interdepartmental relations since production has dealings with many other functions and is often dependent on them.

Now against this background the interesting thing is that there appears to be rather less of this inter-departmental friction in companies in the Netherlands. It cannot of course be wholly absent, and the contrast suggested here is one of degree. First, there do not appear to be any Dutch studies along the lines of the British ones; this tends to suggest that it is not a problem area. Second, I have not been able to unearth any hostile stereotypes or commonly accepted inter-departmental pejoratives: if they exist they are not paraded as in Britain and France. Third, in interviewing Dutch production managers and asking them about any operating difficulties or constraints on output, inadequate support from other departments or friction with them was seldom mentioned—though these responses have been a well-documented theme in British manufacturing.

Mobility between Companies

Dutch management is characterized by low mobility between companies, or, to put it in simpler terms, Dutch managers do not often move from one company to another. Though formal comparative data are hard to come by, the testimony from interviewees on this point is little short of unanimous, and there is no shortage of explanations. First, the regionalism described in Chapter 2, reinforced in some cases by confessional differences or their social heritage, acts as a constraint on the willingness of managers to undertake a change of company which involves a geographical move. It is also commonly asserted in the Netherlands that blue-collar workers are highly immobile geographically—though this view may owe a little to middle-class prejudice. Second, and most important, it is not done; it conflicts with pervasive Dutch notions of loyal service and what people owe to corporate employers. Several informants suggested that more than two moves between companies sounds flighty and will give rise to raised eyebrows. Third, as suggested earlier, the Dutch management ethos does not include an unqualified acceptance of the manager as generalist, so what moves there are between companies tend to be within industries. This puts a natural limit on inter-company mobility: you might move from, say, BP to Shell, or in the chemical industry from DMS to AKZO, but where would you go next? And where would you go on leaving Philips, effectively the only indigenous employer of graduates in electronics. Fourth, pension rights have not been transferable, and this is taken very seriously. Until the late 1980s, when a manager moved from Company A to Company B, they kept their accrued pension entitlement from Company A, but it was not adjusted upwards to take account of inflation as it would have been if they had stayed put.

There are some qualifications which should be made to this picture of low inter-company mobility associated with low geographical mobility. The multinational companies obviously move people geographically and sometimes internationally, whether or not this is part of a career development plan. The multinationals also affect the mobility pattern in another way. Although they naturally recruit direct from the universities and the HBO colleges, some of them also engage in what might be called 'secondary recruitment' in the sense of tempting in other companies' graduates and qualified manpower when they have acquired a bit of experience. There is thus some one-way movement of managers, typically in their early thirties, into the big multinationals.

Again, the generally low company mobility is subject to some local or particular determinants. Owner occupancy rates are high in the Netherlands at 44 per cent as of the late 1980s (though this is low by British standards), and changes in house prices may affect willingness to move. As a particular example, people who bought houses in the 1978–9 period will be reluctant to move because prices peaked at this time and actually declined subsequently. Again, it is much easier, economically, to move from the west to the east since property prices are significantly higher in the west. Finally, notwithstanding all that has been said on the subject of low mobility—and it seems to have been a critical *cause célèbre* in writing about Dutch management—the general view is that there has been some change in the late 1980s, a point that will be taken up in the next chapter.

Dutch management also tends to 'grow its own timber'. This generalization of course relates strongly to the previous observations concerning inter-company mobility. Three points were suggested to me in interviews in the Netherlands in the late 1980s. First is the general one that Dutch companies, and especially the larger ones, are inclined to promote internally and fill most or all positions in this way. Second, this trend is projected further in some large companies by appointing former senior executives to the *raad van commissarissen* (supervisory board, described in Chapter 2). Third, the (especially American) idea that the very top man should come from without, that the head of General Motors should come from Ford, so to speak, is much less acceptable in the Netherlands.

Not by Bread Alone

Most of the evidence from the 1980s suggests that by international standards Dutch managers are underpaid. There are some EC data,[1] the point is made by Anton Buys in the study cited in connection with the status relatives of different functions (Buys, 1985), and it also emerges from a joint survey of the NCD (Netherlands Centrum van Direkteuren) and Hay Management Consultants (NCD–Hay, 1985), supplemented by salary data from other countries in which Hay consultants operate. It should be said that the reference is to net pay, not gross remuneration, and that the relevant sources claim to control for cost of living differences. The NCD–Hay report is quite declaratory on this subject:

Dutch gross salaries lie around the average for all levels of management responsibility in comparison with other Western countries. But through the high levels of taxation and deductions in the Netherlands, this picture changes appreciably when it comes to net salaries. Dutch *net* salaries are lower than in other Western countries. The position of Dutch directors has furthermore deteriorated in this respect in the last two years. (NCD–Hay, 1985; author's translation)

In short, things are bad and getting worse. The NCD–Hay comparison countries are West Germany and Switzerland, which are on top, Belgium, the USA, Italy, Spain, and Britain. Dutch managers are held to be worse paid, net, than managers in all of these. This is damning evidence, but is it significant?

It may well be the case that the 'relative deprivation' of Dutch executives is a fact but an unimportant one; certainly there is an interesting comparison with Sweden, whose managers are also undoubtedly under-remunerated by international comparison. In Sweden (not included in the NCD–Hay evidence) low salary differentiation and high direct taxation continue to render Swedish managers among the poorest in the industrialized world (Lawrence, 1982), a fact that is universally recognized in that country: Swedish managers practically line up for the pleasure of moaning about it to an interested foreigner.

Not so in the Netherlands, where about half the interviewees tell you it is not the case, or they have never thought about it. This tends to confirm the suggestion canvassed earlier that material motivation may be less important for Dutch managers, or perhaps that there is a greater corresponding emphasis on security. One interviewee, a consultant whose work includes putting in stock option and incentive schemes, told me that Dutch managers are often rather put out by this, and respond in a hurt way saying, 'as though I would work harder just for money'. This again does support the interpretation of the relative unimportance of material motivation.

Indeed Dutch management is probably under-motivated in a general material sense. This is an extension of the previous claim concerning low remuneration, but it refers more to the presentation of the facts than to the facts themselves. If you examine recruitment materials and job advertisements in Holland they say little on the subject of remuneration and material rewards. Typically management job advertisements do not mention pay at all, or simply say that pay will be according to the CAO. There is usually no reference to fringe benefits; they are in any case 'thin on the ground' by British standards, and the phrase itself is not easy to render in Dutch. Folklore has it that it is considered bad form in the Netherlands to ask too much about pay at job interviews and that there is relatively little room for bargaining. There is also general agreement that the in-service manager does not use personal achievement, even outstanding achievement, as a lever to ask for a rise: very un-Dutch. In short, differential material motivation does not seem to play a conspicuous part in the motivation of the rank and file of Dutch managers.

Hire but not Fire

Dutch companies tend to be slow to sanction poor performance, at any rate in terms of the ultimate sanction of dismissal. Again interviewees were in general agreement on this issue. Dutch companies do not like to fire people, for two reasons. First, it is un-Dutch: it involves making judgements about people as individuals and violating corporate security expectations. Second, it is expensive. Firing managers is legally and procedurally complicated, and it costs a lot in compensation. As one consultant put it: 'For a manager earning f 100,000–120,000 it costs about f 700,000 to fire him.' But the morality of dismissal is probably the decisive consideration. The conviction that it is wrong to judge individuals *qua* individuals runs deep in the Netherlands. Where else would you meet an ex-accountant who claimed in conversation with me: 'I gave it up because I did not like the idea of criticizing others and judging their actions that auditing involves'?

Learning from Foreigners

At several points we have drawn attention to the internationalism of the Dutch, and their powers of adaptation abroad, both linguistic and social. This does not, however, mean that the Dutch are especially influenced by foreigners or given to the view that they have a lot to learn from foreign management. In part this phenomenon is circumstantial. Let us start in Europe.

The Dutch are unlikely to feel there is anything to learn from the Belgians, even though the latter have been very successful in attracting foreign investment, together with the employment it brings. Dutch views of Belgium seem to be conditioned by the fact that the area that is today Belgium failed to win independence from Spain in the Eighty Years' War (1568–1648), when the Dutch won their independence. The Dutch view of Belgium is not hostile exactly, but a little patronizing and amused. Dutch jokes about the Belgians (there are a lot of them) focus on their presumed silliness, gullibility, and gaucheness.

Or again, whatever the virtues of German management, or the compelling strengths of the German economy, the Dutch simply dislike them too much for the question of learning from them to arise. Dutch sufferings under German occupation (1940–45) during the Second World War have been well documented (van der Zee, 1982), and are firmly imprinted on the folk memory. The result, understandable but regrettable, is a marked tendency to stereotype

German management as bureaucratic, status-conscious, hierarchical, and authoritarian.

The Dutch attitude to France and French management is a little puzzling. While you might have thought that the strengths of French management and the achievements of the post-war French economy would command respect and at least merit serious discussion, the Dutch view seems to be that France is so foreign, so far away culturally, that it is simply not an issue. It is an odd position in view of the geographical closeness of the two countries, especially when you consider the structural similarities of their economies, including inter-war economic stagnation, late industrialization, spectacular economic growth in the post-war period, and strong agriculture and energy sectors.

If you look further afield the Dutch do not seem to share the British view that the Americans are the exemplars of managerial best practice. Dutch managers tend to criticize American management for its short-term outlook and excessive concern with profitability, to dislike the 'hire and fire' mentality, and to find American dynamism and macho decision-making (slightly distasteful) and certainly inappropriate to European conditions. The tide probably changed a little in favour of American precepts and professionalism in the late 1980s, but there is still no general 'looking up' to America in the way that was common in Britain for the quarter century after the Second World War.

The Dutch have also reacted less sharply to the Japanese triumphs than have either the British or the Americans. Dutch interest in Japan is anthropological rather than managerial: yes, Japan is an interesting country, obviously different from Europe and clearly very successful economically, but *so* different from Europe that the question of learning from them with regard to management practice or economic policy scarcely arises. While Dutch managers might take seriously particular Japanese techniques or institutions—say JIT (Just in Time), materials management, or quality circles—the Dutch do not share the view, quite strong in the USA, that there may well be more general things to learn from Japan in such soft and diffuse areas as corporate culture, personal style, decision-making processes, and so on.

If you generalize from these cases a consistent picture emerges. Dutch management is not smug, but there is a feeling that the Netherlands is different and special, so that the practice and example of other countries simply do not impinge very much. It is an interesting concomitant of Dutch internationalism. The Dutch abroad are keen to learn about rather than to learn from.

European Conditionality

At several points we have drawn attention to Dutch restraint and the ability to handle the complicated and conditional, including unusual organizational forms, dialogue with the OR (*order-nemingsraad* or works council), the negotiation of CAOs, liaising with a *verzuild* or pillarized trade union movement; the Dutch willingly become involved in pan-national initiatives and organizations, are able to handle cross-border mergers and joint ventures, and so on. It is worth pausing for a moment and considering the implications of all this for the issue raised in the previous section, the question of learning from abroad.

Take as a practical example the Douwe Egberts company headquartered in Utrecht. It is an old, established Dutch company, very much a household name in the Netherlands; its products include coffee and tea, biscuits and confectionary, dry groceries, pipe and own-roll tobacco, and a range of personal care products. Douwe Egberts is now owned by the Sara Lee Corporation of Chicago, and it is an interesting partnership.

First, there is a business rationale for the association. Douwe Egberts is already dominant in the Dutch market, a dominance enhanced by the acquisition of the van Nelle company, also strong in coffee and tobacco. To start from scratch in new markets in other countries is slow and costly, so an inernational partnership makes sense.

Second, Douwe Egberts is no 'mere subsidiary' of Sara Lee. In 1988 Sara Lee reorganized into five main product lines, and Douwe Egberts represents two of these. That is to say, Douwe Egberts has strategic importance for Sara Lee, is an integral part of the overall business, and enjoys a certain security. This integrality is, among other things, signalled by the fact that the current (1990) Douwe Egberts head Cor Boonstra is a member of the Sara Lee board.

Also of interest in this connection is the fact that at the time of the acquisition of Douwe Egberts by Sara Lee a special trust was set up in the Netherlands. Sara Lee was allowed to move from a 33 per cent to a 100 per cent shareholding, but did not get all the voting rights. Instead Douwe Egberts got a special constitutional arrangement whereby most of these voting rights were vested in the trust referred to above. This trust is staffed by Dutch nationals, and the assumption is that they will not act against specifically Dutch interests. The trust members are all eminent people, and include a former prime minister.

This trust arrangement was negotiated by Cor Boonstra's predecessor at the time of the acquisition. It would probably be fair to say that Cor Boonstra is seen in the Netherlands as representing American vigour and professionalism; as wanting to get the operational things right, to have proper controls, to meet targets. He speaks respectfully of the challenge faced by American business in its homeland, the challenge of organizing distribution, of serving a vast domestic market. Yet Boonstra's thoughts on comparative decision-making in Europe and in the USA, expressed in a conversation with me, are very pertinent:

In Europe when you make decisions you are playing on three chess boards; in the USA only one. In the Netherlands a decision is taken in the *raad van bestuur* (management board). The decision is passed to the *raad van commissarissen* (supervisory board). It is cleared with the OR (works council). It will be communicated direct to the trade unions too. And in our case there will be dialogue with Sara Lee. If you have a more complex task, you learn more. You end up with better management.

It may be that the critical factor in considering the Dutch orientation to business practice in other countries is not being different but having an intelligent awareness of this difference.

Note

[1] I was shown these in one of the interviews but was not told the source.

8

More than a Moment in Time

THE 1980s were an important time in the development of the Netherlands. This is true with regard to Dutch life generally, and with reference to industry and management in particular. The 1980s saw some changes of emphasis. Let us start with the political.

The CDA, the centre Christian party described in Chapter 2, has been in power continuously since the end of the Second World War. That is to say, it has been a member of every coalition government in that period. But in 1981 it formed a coalition with the relatively new centre–right liberal party, the VVD (again see Chapter 2). This, combined with the onset of the world recession in the early 1980s, inaugurated a new political agenda.

This incipient change was consolidated by a new general election in 1982 which confirmed the CDA–VVD coalition in power and led to CDA leader Ruud Lubbers becoming Prime Minister. The same parties 'won' the 1986 election, so the coalition partnership and the prime-ministership of Lubbers were extended into the second half of the decade. In 1989 the two coalition parties fell into disagreement when the VVD rejected some aspects of what was essentially a CDA plan to protect and improve the material environment (*milieubeleidsplan*). This brought down the government, and led to new elections in September 1989, with the result that a new coalition, of the CDA and PvdA (Labour Party), came to power. Ruud Lubbers is still Prime Minister (spring 1990), and much respected. From the outside at least, the new coalition does not seem to have changed direction significantly—at least not yet.

Ruud Lubbers is from Rotterdam and a businessman, and both simple facts are significant. Lubbers represents the down-to-earth, no-nonsense, good-housekeeping, earn a guilder before you spend a guilder propensity in the Dutch make-up. The start of his premier-

ship marked a break with the idealistic exuberance of the 1970s—
when caring and welfare goals were dominant, with an affluent
public sector, and business and industry were downgraded, at least
by implication. The watchword of the Lubber's administration has
been retrenchment—budgetary restraint, spending cuts, limited
public sector growth, and a reshaping of some institutions in the
light of these precepts. The intention here is to explore for a
moment the issue of budgetary cuts, to look at what has happened
in two specific areas, health and education, and to draw the
implications of all this for industry and management.

Lubbers was the first prime minister in Dutch history to cut
government spending, reduce the budgetary deficit, and lower
taxes—and he did all those things together. He also managed to
exude an air of *sang froid* when, in 1983, 700,000 public sector
workers mobilized in industrial action to protest against expenditure cuts. Lubbers retained confidence in these policies even when
unemployment, in 1983, rose to 830,000, or 16 per cent of the
labour force.

Health Care in the Netherlands

If the foregoing remarks are perhaps too generalized to convey
the new spirit of the 1980s in the Netherlands, consider the change
in thinking with regard to health care provision, culminating in the
Dekker Commission recommendations at the end of the decade.

The CDA–VVD coalition view was clearly that the level of
state intervention in medical care had become excessive and was
blunting market forces by creating disincentives and distortions.
This led to efforts to lower both the level of expenditure and the
state deficit while endeavouring to maintain the 'collective burden'
at a constant level.

The provision of health care in the Netherlands is primarily in
the domain of the private sector and is paid for through insurance
schemes. There is, however, heavy government involvement as it
is the government that plans the location and expansion of health
care facilities and also the budgeting of hospitals. Just over 8 per

cent of Dutch GDP is spent on the provision of health care, but there has been a relative slowdown in recent years. In the financial year 1982/3 health care amounted to 8.6 per cent of GDP, but by 1986–7 it amounted to 8.4 per cent (this may be only two decimal points' difference, but it is still a lot of guilders). In 1989 the reforms proposed by the Dekker Commission were implemented. Again the intention was to strengthen market forces in the health sector. Four central problems were identified:

- fragmented funding
- a lack of incentives to encourage cost-consciousness and efficiency
- inadequate co-ordination of health and social services
- inflexibility of the system due to over-regulation.

The Dekker Commission reforms aimed to introduce a market orientation via the introduction of a basic health care insurance package, covering all major health risks, that was to be available to all citizens irrespective of their individual risk in terms of such factors as age.

A key feature of the new scheme was the freedom it allowed to the insurance companies to negotiate contracts with the various providers of care; so, for example, they can negotiate cost reductions with individual hospitals. On the basis of these cost reductions the insurers are able to gain a competitive advantage and offer lower premiums to their clients. And if such savings in costs lead to lower quality the insured are free to change their insurance company at will. Hospitals obtain finance on the basis of the services provided and not from an all-encompassing budget from the government.

Note in the recent reforms outlined above the concern to embrace market forces—and that in an area that has been an emblem of the caring Netherlands. Nor is this an isolated example.

University Education: the New *Élan*

The 1980s saw a change in the guiding philosophy of the Dutch higher education system that parallels the health care reforms discussed in the previous section. The change has been summarized succinctly by Petersen, who argued that 'The period of growth seems to be over. The university system will have to come to terms with the "three R's" of the 1980s: reduction, reallocation, retrenchment' (Petersen, 1981: 4).

The university sector has had to bear the brunt of government expenditure cuts. In 1982 the Minister of Education agreed on an 8 per cent cut in the budgets of Dutch universities. This process was primarily one of task reallocation between the universities, something which is easier in the Netherlands than in many countries given that six of the universities are all within 80 kilometres of each other in the *Randstad*, these being Erasmus University in Rotterdam, the universities at Leiden and Utrecht, the two in Amsterdam, and the technical university at Delft.

These cuts marked a move away from distributional equality between the institutions and were perhaps a precursor of many of the trends evident in current policy, which aims to identify and encourage excellence. The results of this round of cuts included the merger of three schools of dentistry, the closure of three out of five geology departments, the restructuring of philosophy, and the termination of eight out of thirty-five degree programmes in the social sciences (Ackerman, 1988). After the re-election of the Lubbers government in 1986 there was a new round of cuts that reduced the universities' budget by a further 4 per cent. This cut went under the title of 'selective retrenchment and growth', but the perceived emphasis was on the entrenchment.

In 1988 the *Hoger Onderwijs en Onderzoek Plan* (Higher Education and Research Plan—known as *Hoop*) and the *Wet Hoger Onderwijs en Wettenschappelijke Onderwijs* (Higher Education and Research Act) contained tentative proposals for revising the funding system in the direction of an increased use of output-orientated parameters and the use of 'mission budgets' to finance innovative projects and fund centres of excellence. There were also moves towards 'consumer-driven purchasing power' in higher education in the form of a voucher system where students are allocated a set of vouchers to pay for courses they wish to follow—at particular institutions. These institutions are then funded on the basis of the vouchers spent by students.

The Hoop Act referred to above also introduced a system of periodic peer group and outside expert reviews of the individual universities (and facilities within them). These reviews are to serve as the basis for future growth and retrenchment decisions, and the process also involves the universities in the production of development plans every two years.

Finally, in the revised version of the Hoop Act published in 1990 two other measures have reinforced the market orientation of the Dutch higher education system. The intention of the revised Act is to minimize government interference and to create market conditions for the universities. One way in which this is to be achieved is by means of a publication listing and evaluating the various courses, which will serve as a 'consumers' guide to higher education' as well as creating competition between establishments. This revised Act also introduces a completion component, linking the funding of institutions to the numbers of students who have completed courses rather than to actual enrolments.

Our starting point is that there has been significant change of emphasis and orientation in the Netherlands in the 1980s. The two examples of health care and higher education have been pursued in some detail because they capture the essence of this change. The picture that emerges, with the emphasis on cost-cutting, control, retrenchment, and market forces, is not that of the Netherlands that foreigners think they know. But it was the reality of the 1980s and the new decade does not so far show any sign of change in these matters. The next question concerns the extent to which management has been affected by this 1980s ethos.

Industry and Management in the 1980s

In the earlier characterization of Dutch management there have been a lot of hints that things changed in the 1980s. We have spoken of management behaviour or attitudes as being 'traditionally the case' or as having changed 'only recently' or as being the normal state of affairs 'until the late 1980s'. So the aim here is to offer a more systematic account, and to respond to the question, what exactly changed in the course of the 1980s.

The first thing to emerge was a certain interest in, even sponsorship of, industry that was qualitatively new. The year 1981 saw the publication of the report of the Advisory Commission on Industrial Policy chaired by a former president of Shell. The report was significantly entitled *Een Nieuw Industrieel Elan* ('A New Industrial *Élan*'). Much of the detail of the report is quite dull, apart from an analysis of the areas in which the Netherlands might be held to possess a competitive advantage. But the report has a phenomenological interest: it is replete with celebrations of entrepreneurialism, wealth generation, and managerial virtuosity. These had not been the shibboleths of Dutch affairs in the 1970s.

The Status of Industry

The most important general point to make is that the 1980s saw a rise in the status of industry. At the start of the period industry had a low standing, but at the end of the period it was perceived as 'vital to the nation's interest', the motor of the country's wealth, something worthy of government sponsorship and public respect.

If all this sounds a rather familiar story to British readers it is worth pausing for a moment to consider both the similarity and the uniqueness of this rise in the status of industry. The 1980s seem to have witnessed a rise in the standing of industry throughout the industrialized world. A general revaluation of industry, management, wealth creation, and entrepreneurialism occurred. The development was not unique to the Netherlands, and clearly occurred in Britain as well—nor was it confined to countries like Britain and the Netherlands which moved to the political right around the start of the decade, sharply in 1979 in the British case, more moderately in 1981 in the Dutch case, as described at the start of this chapter. In France, which had an effective socialist administration in the 1981–6 period (and a socialist president beyond that) a similar development is observable: a rise in status and remuneration for *les cadres*, a rehabilitation of the French *patron* (for the first time since the Vichy period of 1940–44), an interest on the part of the general public in business and management, and even a longing for management idols and business heroes (Barsoux and Lawrence, 1990). In West Germany, the most industrialized country in the world, the 1980s also saw an interest in management *per se* (as opposed to *Technik*), a growth of American business forms, and a massive rise in enrolment on undergraduate management courses (strictly speaking, courses in *Betriebswirtschaftslehre* or business economics). In short, the rise in the status of industry in the 1980s was widespread. The Netherlands was not unique in experiencing it, though it is still of interest to note that its experience was part of a wider movement.

At the same time, what happened in the Netherlands is not necessarily exactly the same as what occurred elsewhere. Here the comparison with Britain is instructive, especially if we ask what the rise in the standing of industry was a reaction against. In Britain there had been a long-standing tradition of anti-industrialism, noted alike by British (Barnett, 1972) and foreign observers (Wiener, 1981). Being a country gentleman (who did not 'do' anything) was the ideal, being a colonial administrator was next best thing, if you had to work. Neither the social élite nor the educational élite were attracted to industrial management; among the *noblesse de la robe* the free professions and for that matter jobs in the media were a good deal more attractive than posts in management.

It was against this background of anti-industrialism, suffused with overtones of aspirant aristocracy, that the 1980s revaluation of industry and management occurred in Britain. But very little of this applies to (apparently) the same process in the Netherlands. Until the 1980s the Dutch neglect of industry was a consequence of different ideals and priorities. Once the pressing needs of post-war reconstruction had been met, industry ceased to be prominent.

Government, politics, policy, planning, education all seemed more exciting areas to be involved in than management. Money-making and its practitioners took a back seat in an affluent, caring, spending, idealistic society. And of course you could take growth and prosperity for granted. Back in the 1960s Nobel Prize-winning Dutch economist Jan Timbergen had forecast the ending of the economic cycle and argued that the Netherlands would enjoy 'festoons' of economic growth. Material values of wealth, property, and possessions gave way to post-material values (Inglehart, 1977). This was the background to the Dutch revaluation of industry, spurred by a world recession and rising unemployment, and with a Rotterdam businessman at the national helm. So the change in the Netherlands is not unique, it is part of a wider phenomenon, yet the particular meaning and background to the changes are distinctive.

So far the phenomenon has been depicted in institutional rather than personal terms, yet it has a distinct personal meaning. In the course of the 1980s management became a strong and popular career choice for the most able. In the idealistic euphoria of the 1970s, management had not only been 'not a strong career choice' but a little bit shameful. As a consultant put it to me in a discussion in 1985, in the 1970s 'a kid at school would not want to admit that his father worked in management' (Lawrence, 1986).

Management Behaviour

Against the background of this macro change a range of micro-behavioural changes are noticeable. None of them are black and white affairs, all are gradualist, things that have to be seen in the traditional Dutch context. The first thing is difficult to express except in a rather impressionistic way. It is that broadly speaking companies have 'smartened up their act'. There is a lot of hearsay evidence to the effect that Dutch companies in the 1960s and 1970s were fairly easy-going outfits, that they prospered because of high levels of post-war growth, rather than because of inherent excellence or fierce professionalism. There are also a lot of clues to this effect in the NCD–Hay surveys referred to in Chapter 7. These suggest a growing awareness among managers, as the decade unfolds, of the importance of target-setting, planning, budgeting, reporting, and controls, indeed a general growth in proactive management behaviour.

At a more individual level the 1980s saw a partial and covert legitimization of ambition. Having ambition, wanting to get on, is still not something a good Dutchman will proclaim, but it is now at least quietly acceptable. So in the same way is excellence. Companies are less restrained in the claims they make about themselves, will compete in terms of differentiation rather than conformity. As a consultant put it to me at the end of the decade, 'We are no longer afraid to claim that we are Number One.'

This emergent individualism has been accompanied by a franker interest in remuneration. It is still not Dutch to place a concern with remuneration in the foreground, but at least the issue can be admitted to the agenda. Stock option schemes have become more widespread for senior executives, fringe benefits more acceptable and more sought after at other levels. (In 1985 when I first went to the Netherlands I had to ask several people before finding someone who could give me a Dutch rendering of fringe benefits; now the phrase *secundaire arbeidsvoorwaarden* is common speech, and looms out from the pages of the management job advertisements.)

Attitudes to mobility have softened. The traditional view outlined in Chapter 7, according to which manager mobility was seen as an amalgam of personal disloyalty (to employers), overweening pride, and emotional instability, has now been modified to embrace a qualified appeciation of moderate and sensible mobility between companies.

There is another change in the way that actual or potential managers are esteemed that is more difficult to formulate. Part of it is a greater readiness to admit to individual distinctions, to say that Manager A is better than Manager B. Side by side with this is a more pronounced willingness to recognize the expressly *managerial* component of job performance. The old view somehow seemed to suggest that all that was required was an appropriate qualification crossed with industry-specific knowledge and all would be well. To parody it a little, it went something like this: OK, this is the chemical industry, you have a degree in chemistry and eighteen months' experience in this outfit, and you are a decently modest person, so that is all that is required and you will get it right (and so would anyone else with your attributes). The new view tends to be more managerially discriminating, going beyond the basically qualified and typically experienced to stress the importance of social or political skills, management know-how, or goal internalization.

Words not Deeds

In the earlier characterization of traditional Dutch management we referred to the form and wording of Dutch management job adverts in that they tended to support this characterization. Now we have argued for a change of ethos in the 1980s, and that prompts the question, have the adverts changed, do they reflect the 'new age' of Dutch management? Yes, they have changed, principally in the second half of the 1980s, and the change is in line with the developments outlined in the last few pages. In short management advertisements are now more likely to

- be explicit about remuneration;
- mention fringe benefits;
- engage in corporate 'trumpet-blowing';
- make concessions to the differentiation of status and rewards;
- gently 'trawl' for dynamism and proactivity.

As already seen, the principal source of management job adverts in the Netherlands is the weekly paper *Intermediair*. Against the background of earlier accounts of what constitutes the typical job advert in the Netherlands consider one of the last issues of *Intermediair* for the 1980s, that of 15 December 1989. It provides a nice illustration of several of the points made in this section.

The Intermediair *Job Columns*

The back page of the relevant edition makes a nice starting place for the exercise in hand. Here Ebbinge Consultants have a whole page devoted to job adverts on behalf of their clients, and every one is in the format: job title, followed by salary. For example:

> Manager, Distribution Centre
> 100 à 120,000
> [i.e. a gross annual salary of *c.* £33,000–40,000]

or

> Management Consultant
> Strategy and Finance
> 80 à 110,000
> [i.e. a gross annual salary of *c.* £27,000–37,000]

In other words, they are just like British management job adverts in the *Daily Telegraph*.

Nor are Ebbinge Consultants blazing a lone trail in this, even though you might expect consultants to be more brassy on behalf of their clients than those companies would be on their own account. On page 38, for example, Michael Page International (specialists in financial recruitment) advertise three controller and/or accountant jobs using the same formula—indeed theirs were the first to advertise salary plus car! This may be the British norm, but certainly does not have a long history in the Netherlands. Or again, on page 20, the PA Consulting Group have an advert that reads:

> Operations Manager
> Young production man with international flare
> 100,000 + +

It may seem a small point to British readers but this '+ +' formula is not at all the traditional Dutch way of doing things. Yet first prize in the new order must go to Hewlett-Packard whose advertisement, on page 32, for customer engineers actually had 'The remuneration' as a side heading:

The remuneration

For this job at Hewlett-Packard you can depend on an interesting remuneration. What is more we offer you a works car, profit-sharing, a non-contributory pension, and a stock option scheme.

The Americans just don't know where to stop. A milder version which is common now does not actually name a figure, but gravely hints at a sum of some magnitude. Typical of this new genre is the Talent Search advert (page 22) for an Area Manager in Southern Europe for an agricultural products company: 'The company is offering a dynamic job in an international environment. The remuneration and the fringe benefits are in accord with the importance ance [literally weight] of the function.'

There are other themes. Consider this excerpt from one of the Ebbinge Consultants specifications, the one for the Distribution Centre Manager:

The development of the logistical system/procedures will be effected by the Logistics Manager. The DC [Distribution Centre] manager sought in this advert will report to him. The DC manager is the operational manager. He will be responsible for the work, the workers, and the compatibility of the systems; he will be responsible to the Head of Production, the Head of the Warehouse, ... Furthermore he will have contacts with Sales Managers, Branch Managers, Suppliers, the Head of Personnel, the Head of Administration, and external transport.

What is remarkable about this? Is not just a businesslike Dutch account of what the job involves? Maybe, but it reads very much like a British advert where there is concern to define the job in status and hierarchy terms; in the British scheme of things you know how important a job is by whom you report to, who else's beck and call you are at, how lustrous your contacts are, whether or not you are trusted to represent the organization with outsiders, whether or not there is anyone of importance in the organization who is going to be dependent on you. Out of context this interpretation might not hold, but there is a context here—of gentle convergence between Dutch and British management views.

More is to come. If there is one thing the Dutch dislike, it is boastfulness. And what do we have nowadays but consultants boasting about their clients, companies blowing their own trumpet.

Start with Ebbinge Consultants again. Their first advert is for a general director for the company Nilfisk Nederland, described as 'the local marketing company for a powerful Danish firm, ... counted among the best-known of Danish concerns'. And again: 'The market position [of the company] is strong, the reputation outstanding. It is the market leader in professional cleaning for as long as anyone can remember.'

Another of the Ebbinge Consultants adverts on the same back page describes its client company as

One of the leading deliverers of automatic dispensing machines for catering operations. High tech. orientation. Technology driven marketing. The most modern apparatus is delivered on long-term contracts to among others many of our top companies in the Netherlands.

How intemperate the claims, what status-mongering, how un-Dutch! Even a well-established household name company such as AKZO introduces this advert for a Head of Product Process Quality (page 132) with the claim:

AKZO is one of the greatest chemical concerns of the world, with the head office in Arnhem, with 350 sites in 50 countries, and some 70,000 employees. Working for AKZO means a career with a technologically highly developed company

The claims in these advertisements are perfectly just: the interesting thing is that they have not traditionally been advanced.

Ephemeral or Epochal?

We may have proceeded a little flippantly in the last few pages, but there is a serious issue at stake. This is that our earlier characterization of management in the Netherlands needs to be modified in particular ways to take account of changes in the 1980s. There appears, in short, to be some loss of distinctiveness by Dutch management, some qualified move in terms of attitude and practice towards the Anglo-American norms. This in turn raises the question, how deep do these changes go?

There can be no definitive answer; there are no facts; it can only be a matter of interpretation. I would like to argue it both ways. First, the changes outlined here have to be taken seriously. They have not occurred in a vacuum. In spirit at least they are government-sponsored, and in line with the government's emphasis on economy, control, and market forces. Second, the changed mood and disposition of Dutch management is in part the product of outside forces in the form of the world recession of the early 1980s and the ensuing intensification of competition. Third, some of the changes in the Netherlands are paralleled by developments in other industrial countries and we have briefly considered the case of Britain, France, and West Germany in this matter. Fourth, the management changes are not only influenced loosely speaking by political direction but are also in line with other sectoral changes, and we considered here developments in higher education and health care. What is more, some of the changes in presumed motivation that we illustrated from the *Intermediair* job adverts are also in evidence in the adverts for public sector appointments. In the 'old days' (about 1985!) no public sector job advert would carry a salary; the most one could expect would be a small print note at the end that the salary would be in accordance with the CAO. But in the same edition of *Intermediair* from which the private sector examples have been taken, most of the adverts for public sector, mostly public authority posts state the salary, and some even try to tempt the mercenary by saying what the maximum salary might be.

There is another broad reason for taking seriously the idea that the changes described above are 'here to stay'. The underlying assumption is that the internationalism of business and management, underpinned by the power of the media, makes national distinctiveness difficult to sustain. So if management in a country 'steps out of line' you might expect this to be only temporary, that forces of international interdependence will bring it back to normal. The reverse proposition is that when a country's management takes a step away from distinctiveness, and towards the international norm, there will be no turning back. Once Dutch personnel officers have appealed to the material aspirations of potential applicants, just like personnel officers in other countries, there will be no return.

There are at least two counter-arguments. The first is that these 1980s developments do run counter to Dutch tradition and disposition, so their acceptance may always be conditional, less than whole-hearted. This phenomenon is often clear in discussion with Dutch managers in which they will say what modern practice is, and then indicate that they have reservations about it. On one such occasion a consultant told me how attitudes to mobility between companies had changed and then added: 'Of course, when I get an application from someone who has had three jobs or more I know they're unstable. I earmark them for our "turn-around' division" ' (that is, short-term assignments with ailing companies).

Indeed the mobility issue is perhaps a good test case, with its implications for a range of interlocking Dutch values. Consider the case of Paul Snoep, who attained the status of executive black celebrity. Paul Snoep was a senior manager at Heineken, at the level immediately below that of the board (*raad van bestuur*). He left Heineken to take a board-level position at Douwe Egberts. Then two years later he moved again to the top position in the brewery Grolsch. Now this is admittedly not a run-of-the-mill case of inter-company mobility. Yet the story started in 1984: in 1989 every single Dutch manager with whom I raised the question of manager mobility regaled me with the Paul Snoep story.

The second counter-argument is that the changes are not absolute, the transition is not a black and white affair. Rather there is a dilution, not a displacement, of Dutch management practice, an intermingling of old and new strands. Again this intermingling could be abundantly illustrated from contemporary job advertisements and job descriptions. As a single example consider this advert for the post of Head of Purchasing at the Venlo-based stationery company, Enfa BV, taken from the same edition of *Intermediair*. The advertisement includes a section:

Enfa offers:

- the opportunity to use your experience to develop this department

- a many-sided purchasing operation with interesting technical aspects
- a human-orientated company with an informal atmosphere and loyal colleagues
- the opportunity to make an important contribution to higher quality and lower costs
- a good salary as well as decent fringe benefits.

Here we have the traditional appeal to intrinsic satisfactions and the value placed on work climate, 'topped off' with assurances about remuneration. The thrust of this last line of argument is that we should perhaps think of the changes of the 1980s as an exercise in grafting rather than in substitution.

9

The Flying Dutchman

HEINEKEN and Grolsch, the two leading breweries of the Netherlands, were discussed in Chapter 1 to illustrate the themes of
internationalism and imagination. In this final chapter we will round
off by considering another leading Dutch company, the airline
KLM. This immediately raises the question as to what KLM illustrates. There are several answers. KLM exemplifies a Dutch strength
in the provision of services. It offers in the person of its founder
an instance of a Dutch hero in a nation not prone to hero worship.
Finally, it illustrates the Dutch ability to handle complexity, to do
a number of resourceful and intelligent things at the same time, in
a situation marked by some threat and much uncertainty, and to
do this with more than moderate success. We will put the emphasis
on the last of these, but all three themes are worth airing.

Service Industry in the Netherlands

In an earlier chapter we pointed to the preponderance of service
rather than manufacturing industries in the Netherlands. The same
idea is advanced in more general terms by Geert Hofstede in
his inaugural lecture at the University of Limburg in Maastricht.
Building on the 'masculine' (assertive, dominant, leading, goal-
setting) versus 'feminine' (caring, nurturing, valuing relationships
rather than outcomes) dimensions developed in his earlier work
(Hofstede, 1980), Hofstede says of the Dutch:

In comparison with our neighbour countries and obvious trade partners,
our culture distinguishes itself primarily by its feminity. Under conditions
of free international competition—a relatively recent phenomenon in
our world, and one which is still under a constant threat of national
protectionism—a country will maintain the strongest economic position

in those fields to which it possesses a cultural affinity. For a masculine country this is primarily the production of goods: making them well, in large quantities, and efficiently. For a feminine country like the Netherlands, this is the rendering of services, in which the relationship with the customer is essential: trade, banking, consulting, health care, transport; but also the production of like products, which have to be grown, that is nurtured, rather than produced: intensive agriculture, animal husbandry, biochemistry. Whoever looks at the pattern of economic activity in the Netherlands will notice that these are precisely the fields in which we compete quite successfully. (Hofstede, 1987: 11)

In the case of KLM, however, it is not simply a matter of the Dutch proclivity for service provision. A certain pioneering spirit, Dutch internationalism, and, as we hope to demonstrate, a sustained business resourcefulness, all combine in a company that is a national emblem as well as a national airline.

KLM at Large

KLM, as we have shown, is the twelfth largest (private sector) employer in the Netherlands with 23,932 employees as of March 1987. It is also the twelfth largest company in terms of turnover, coming just after Heineken and just ahead of Koninklijke Nedloyd Groep (a shipping company).

The Netherlands has a favourable trade balance. Transport is a significant contributor to this favourable balance, more so than in most European countries, and KLM plays a key role in this. It also measures up on the world stage. In 1989 there were 185 airlines with membership of IATA. Figures for the previous year show that by the industry measure of ton-kilometres KLM was in twelfth place in the world league. This overall ton-kilometre measure is, however, a little unfair to the European airlines, and especially the small country airlines, where the domestic mileage does not amount to much. To put it the other way round, this global criterion favours the USA, with its vast domestic network: United Airlines comes top, American Airlines is second; indeed American companies have seven out of the top twelve places.

If we turn to the measure of *international* ton-kilometres the relativities are changed in favour of Europe and KLM holds sixth place in the world league. The actual order is instructive (see table below).

Six largest airlines by international ton-kilometres for 1988

British Airways	7,046m.
Japan Airlines	6,994m.
Lufthansa	6,607m.
Air France	5,438m.
Pan American	4,329m.
KLM	4,108m.

NB: The Netherlands is the only small country whose airline is represented in this top six league table (and the same applies to the top twelve league by overall ton-kilometres).

Source: IATA statistics.

Schipol Airport

Schipol, the Netherlands' main airport just outside Amsterdam and KLM's base, has a similar standing. In 1988 Schipol held fifth place among European airports for number of passengers handled, coming after London, Paris, Frankfurt, and Rome. In the same year it held fourth place in Europe for volume of freight handled, coming after Frankfurt, London, and Paris.

Everyone likes Schipol. It has the great merit of being a one-terminal airport where passengers can reach all of it on foot on one level (compare London's Heathrow and Paris's Charles de Gaulle with their inter-terminal buses). Schipol has automated baggage handling and a nice shopping centre, and Schipol railway station not only gives a convenient link with central Amsterdam but is also a regular stop on the inter-city route from Rotterdam

and The Hague to Amsterdam—that is, it is part of the national
network not just a spur.

The present Schipol was opened in 1968, planned on a generous
scale, the product of earlier vision. In consequence it has not
suffered the acute capacity problems that have plagued some of
the other European airports. In the early 1990s Schipol is being
substantially enlarged, but without any perceptible disruption.
Clearly Amsterdam will continue to be served by a single airport,
unlike London and Paris, or even Stockholm. Schipol is reckoned
to be the best hub airport in the world (see p. 168).

These various claims to fame tend to prompt a single question:
how did it all start?

The World's Oldest Airline

A lot of countries founded airlines around the end of the First
World War, but KLM's claim to fame is that it has always existed
under the same name, in full Koninklijke Luchtvaart Maatschappij.
Compare this continuity with, for instance, the various manifes-
tations of Britain's national airline from Imperial Airways to BEA/
BOAC to British Airways.

KLM was founded on 7 October 1919 by Albert Plesman.
Plesman was a young officer pilot in the Dutch airforce who used
the platform of the first aeronautical show in Amsterdam, the ELTA
of 1919, to promote his vision of a commerical exploitation of
aircraft. He was KLM's first president from then until his death on
New Year's Eve 1953. The first flight had to wait until 17 May
1920 (because of the winter) and was from London to Amsterdam
in a De Havilland DH-9 which carried two passengers. At this time
passengers were issued with a leather coat, flying helmet, goggles,
gloves, and a scarf—with a hot water bottle if the weather was
really cold.

From the start KLM flew both passengers and freight. It was
also active at an early stage in aerial mapping, and formed a
subsidiary KLM Aerocarto (most of it sold off in 1989). In 1924
KLM staged an experimental flight to the Dutch East Indies (now

Indonesia), and in 1927 it opened a regular Amsterdam–Jakarta service. In 1934 it introduced all-metal aircraft by acquiring the Douglas DC-2. The first of these aircraft delivered to KLM—the PH-AJU 'Uiver'—immediately became famous by gaining first place in the handicap category in the 1934 London–Melbourne Race. Again in 1936 KLM was the first European airline to have the legendary DC-3, better known as the Dakota of Second World War fame.

Indeed, throughout its life KLM has had a number of firsts, especially with regard to aircraft acquisition. KLM was very quick off the mark at the end of the war, despite the devastation of Schipol airport, which had more than 200 bomb craters on its runway in May 1945. KLM was in fact the first European airline to inaugurate a regular service with the USA in 1946. It was also the first European airline to operate the Douglas DC-9 (1966), and the first in the world to operate the Boeing 747B (1971), heavier and with a longer range than the original 747. It was similarly first (1972) with the DC-10-30, the longer-range version of the DC-10, first in 1975 with the 747M, and in 1989 first in Europe to operate the Boeing 747-400. These are only some of the 'commanding heights' but KLM has in general been a pioneer, and not only in the early stages of the industry's development.

A Dutch Hero

Albert Plesman got away to a good start as a Dutch hero by having humble origins. He was born in 1889 in The Hague where his parents had a grocery shop. One biographer observes with approval: 'As members of the *petite bourgeoisie* [*kleine middenstanders* in the original Dutch, which has a more positive ring to it] his parents lived an unremarkable life marked by early rising and hard work' (Leeuw, 1989: 9). The young Albert helped with door-to-door deliveries and it was later a family joke with his own children that if he had simply inherited his parents' shop his natural drive would have turned it into an Albert Heijn chain (Ahold, the owner of the Albert Heijn chain, is the sixth largest Dutch company by turnover). He did not distinguish himself at school, and on one occasion had to repeat a year. He also stuttered as a schoolboy, though he later overcame the difficulty. Again René de Leeuw sums up his school performance with the remark: 'With regard to his feeling for language and written style his teachers were unenthusiastic, though he stood out in arithmetic. But with his powerful physique he soon surpassed most of his contemporaries in sport' (Leeuw, 1989: 10).

The bigness is a constant theme, literally and figuratively. Photographs show a tall, big-framed man, with a sense of purpose. Colleagues speak of a man who was bluff, forceful, and decent. If he had been English he would have been a Yorkshireman, unadorned in speech, direct in manner, and quite unpretentious. He was happily married, and a strong family man; there was never a hint of scandal or corruption. Everyone seems to have liked and respected him, except the German authorities during the Occupation who suspected him of some act of sabotage and eventually rusticated him to Overijssel province in the east (his son Jan escaped to England in 1940 and became a fighter pilot with the RAF's 322 squadron; he was later shot down and killed on a raid at St Omer—Plesman's worst blow during the awful war years).

Plesman was much given to pithy sayings, some of which have been collected and preserved in Leeuw's biography. They are sometimes a bit difficult to translate, or at least you have to translate freely to try to capture the spirit of them. For instance: *'Voor een raar bedrijf heb je raar volk nodig'* ('For an exceptional company you need exceptional people'), or *'Wie ben je en wat doe je?—Doe maar goed je best'* ('Whoever you are and whatever your job is, do it well!') or *'Alles wat je met liefde doet, slaagt'* ('Everything you do with passion and conviction succeeds').

In his pioneering role at KLM his two most striking qualities were energy and vision. He founded the airline and for more than thirty years he ran it. Most of the triumphs and *démarches* described in the previous section are his. It took some drive and decision to inaugurate a 55-day experimental flight from Amsterdam to the East Indies in 1924, some independence of mind to switch from Anthony Fokker's excellent series of planes to the American all-metal, pressurized fuselage models in the early 1930s. Indeed, it took vision to grasp all the possibilities from the start—passengers, post, freight, aerial mapping.

The one occasion when it might all have been lost through demoralization and a delayed recovery at the end of the war in fact proved to be perhaps Plesman's greatest triumph. When the British liberated the eastern city of Enschede, Plesman promptly set out from his home in a nearby village to make contact with the liberators. He importuned the British army into providing a jeep and a driver, and dashed down to Eindhoven in the south; Eindhoven had been liberated in September 1944 in the Arnhem offensive and served as a sort of headquarters for the liberated part of the country from then on. At Eindhoven he conferred with Prince Bernhard and confided his intention of going to the USA. There was one thing America had more of than anyone else: aeroplanes.

Plesman reached Washington, via London and Bristol, and had two meetings with the American Airforce commander-in-chief and even a session with President Harry Truman (Plesman is reported to have spoken a forceful rather than a stylish English). He got his aeroplanes: eighteen four-engine DC-4 skymasters and thirty Dakotas. It cannot have been easy to prise these planes out of the American government, still at war with Japan, but Plesman did it.

The post-war start-up was remarkable. First internal flights were resumed, then, within six months of the end of the war, flights to Jakarta. On 21 May 1946 KLM started flights to the USA—as noted in the previous section, the first European airline to do so. At this date the war had been over for the Netherlands for one year and sixteen days.

One of Plesman's sayings is to the effect that if you were able to say something at the time of your death it would be nice to be able to claim '*Ik heb ieder het zijne gegeven, ik heb iets tot stand gebracht, sluit de kist.* The sense is something like: 'I have given everyone their due, I brought one or two things to fruition, O.K. close the lid' (a Dutch epitaph).

Change and Challenge

At the end of the 1980s the airline industry seemed a very attractive one. The period witnessed industry growth, increases in traffic and yield, and, in 1988, the best financial results in the industry's history. In that year the overall profit of IATA carriers nearly doubled to $1.5 billion (van Wijk, 1989). So where is the change and challenge?

First, there is the effect of American deregulation in the 1970s. This, basically, led to a shake-out (of the weak or inefficient), to concentration, and to a move towards internationalization, at least on the part of those American airlines with a strong domestic position, airlines such as Delta or United. US deregulation and its aftermath led to a change in the 'balance of power' among American airlines. The ones with strong domestic bases gained, while the 'old-fashioned' ones, Pan Am and TWA, experienced a relative decline.

What is more, at the end of the deregulation process if not at its beginning, American airlines became stronger *vis à vis* European ones, and more predatory. Bear in mind that the USA has the biggest domestic network and more airports than any other country in the world, and that all American airlines can at least in principle use all these airports, while European airlines can use only a few of them, and their operation is circumscribed by 'air political' considerations. In contrast, post-deregulation US airlines have not been correspondingly handicapped in their flights to and from Europe; more city-pair routes have emerged as a result of deregu-lation, and the American airlines have bypassed European gateway airports when it has suited them, or tried to develop their own European hubs—London and Frankfurt for Pan Am, Paris for TWA. One ready indicator of the Euro-American balance of power is the relative share of the north Atlantic routes. In 1986 the US carriers had a 44 per cent share; the projected figure for 1989 was 54 per cent (van Wijk, 1989). In short, as a result of deregulation some six US mega-carriers have survived and made the world their battlefield.

Second, there is the threat from the Far East carriers, particularly

Cathay Pacific and Singapore Airlines. They have enjoyed enormous market growth, combining high quality service, creative advertising, and a low cost structure. In 1970 Cathay only carried half a million passengers a year, but by 1989 this had reached well over 5 million—an annual growth of around 15 per cent (van Wijk, 1989).

Third, there is 1992 and the Single European Market. It is important, but it breeds a certain insecurity. At the moment European airlines cannot fly everywhere they choose on an intra-Europe basis; it is all limited by negotiations and agreements. But will this change in 1992, and in particular will European airlines be able to fly between 'third party' points (could KLM offer a service between Frankfurt and Lyon, for example)? No one knows for certain. And if the answer turns out to be yes, this means that 'air political' constraints will have been removed, but the logistical restriction of available slots (a slot is the right to use an air-lane and a runway at a particular time) will be more critical. And if this is so, should not every European airline) be trying to establish themselves as widely as possible in the run-up to 1992?

Fourth, there is the little matter of air traffic control problems. At the end of the 1980s 25 per cent of all flights in Europe were delayed by a quarter of an hour or more because of air traffic control factors. This is bad news for passengers, and especially holiday-making passengers. It also blurs the punctuality performance of airlines, and restricts the use of punctuality–reliability as a competitive weapon.

This is far from being an exhaustive analysis of the state of the airline industry, but enough has been said to show that this is not an industry for the slow, the weak, or the unready. This raises the question: how has KLM fared? We will deliberately give an answer that is in part middle term, in the sense of looking back a little over KLM's history, as well as thinking about the future.

Moving Things

To start with, KLM has always had a strong sense of core business, and this means passengers *and* freight. The latter may not be so glamorous, but at the end of the 1980s freight accounted for some 46 per cent of the volume and 18 per cent of the revenue. One of the airline's publications lists the 'most important categories of freight' (KLM, 1989):

- newspapers and magazines
- computers
- meat, fruit, and vegetables
- living animals
- cut flowers and plants, bushes and shrubs
- books and printed matter
- clothing and manufactured goods
- textiles and leather goods
- machines, components, tools
- vehicles, parts, and accessories
- sound, electronic, and communication equipment
- scientific instruments
- optical and photographic equipment
- footwear
- chemical, pharmaceutical, and cosmetic products
- mechanical and electronic office equipment

It is a fascinating list, universalism crossed with Dutch specialities.

Freight, it should be said, has been revolutionized more in the 1980s than passengers travel. Freight transportation has generated new markets: the JIT market, where the exact time of delivery is important; and the door-to-door market, which involves integrating air and road transport. In freight the competitive weapon these days is logistics; the gains are made on the ground, with electronic data processing, and expedited documentation, an idea developed earlier in the brief discussion of road haulage in the Netherlands. KLM also has a share (34.7 per cent) in the Venlo-based trucking firm, Frans Maas—a common-sense development for an airline engaged in freight transportation.

There is a further aspect to the freight operation. This is that KLM has been a leader in the use of combi aircraft. A combi is a plane that carries both passengers and freight; the planes used in this way by KLM are modified DC-10s and 747s. The point is to raise the load factor, and thereby spread the costs: better a combi plane nearly full with a mix of passengers and freight, than one half empty with either. A further advantage of the use of combis is that some airports cannot handle the biggest planes because they cannot cope with a full payload of passengers from a 747. Here the combi tactic gets you into such an airport with half a payload of passengers, which is acceptable to the receiving airport, but with a full-capacity big plane, which is desirable for the carrier.

Third Party Services

At the start of the chapter we mentioned a number of KLM firsts in terms of route starts and new aeroplane acquisitions. There is another: KLM was the first airline in the world to train flight attendants. This was not something that happened in the 1980s, with its Tom Peters-led 'close to the customer' emphasis (Peters and Austin, 1985). Nor was it a response to competition from the Far East airlines, or inspired by the Japanese quality revolution. Training attendants started for KLM in 1935, and this is indicative.

Training has become a KLM strength. It is not only training its own staff, but doing training over a wide range of jobs for a variety of other airlines. KLM also offers technical maintenance services to other airlines. Indeed it has a specialized capability for the maintenance of Boeing 747s, together with their General Electric CF-6 aero-engines. If you add to these training and technical maintenance services the catering provision, handling charges, and sale of automatic systems and management services to other airlines, this represents a substantial source of income. For the financial year 1988/9 revenue for these services to third parties amounted to ƒ944 million (more the £300 million).

Hubs, Spokes and Strategies

It has been shown that deregulation in the USA led to concentration and facilitated the emergence of hubs. A hub is an airport with a disproportionate number of flights (the spokes) and probably served by a more than average number of airlines. Hubs are often where passengers change flights. Since not all desired destinations are directly linked you may fly from A to the hub and then on to B, not direct from A to B. Hubs may also facilitate intercontinental links on a two-step flow model. So you may fly from somewhere in Kansas or Nebraska to Kansas City, and then direct to a European destination. Or you might arrive in Denver from Tokyo and then fly on to Seattle. Where does all this leave KLM and Schipol?

Schipol is actually well placed as an intercontinental hub. First, it is in the right place in Europe, that is to say, it is in the most economically dense 'square', whose corners are Frankfurt, Paris, London, and Amsterdam. Second, KLM is favoured by its traditional strength in intercontinental routes, transatlantic and Far Eastern. And long routes are in turn desirable since the further an aeroplane goes the lower the cost per unit of distance: in KLM's case this is particularly desirable given a high cost structure resulting from high wage levels and social security provision in the Netherlands. Third, Schipol is an ideal hub airport as it has plenty of capacity, good ground connections, and a single terminal system which makes it easy for passengers to change planes. On the other hand, it is open to competition, and, as hinted earlier, it is threatened by the US mega-carriers who may try to create their own hubs in Europe and bypass European gateways. What has KLM been doing?

The KLM–Schipol hub is sustained in various ways:

- by the capacity and attractiveness of Schipol;
- by KLM subsidiary NLM City Hopper feeding KLM–Schipol with smaller aircraft;
- by having equity stakes in airlines flying from other countries into Schipol, specifically the Belgian regional Delta Airlines and Air UK; KLM has a 14.9 per cent stake in Air UK and underwrites its acquisition of aircraft.

This development is also assisted by the special relationship between the Netherlands and Britain, who liberalized their air relations in the mid-1980s. That is to say, they totally liberalized the market—routes, frequency, price, and access to destinations. This is a unique development in the industry, and led to a doubling of traffic in four years. One result is that Schipol is now connected to more destinations in the UK than is Heathrow.

KLM seems to be well-positioned in some other ways. It is not itself a charter airline, but it has a share in Transavia (40 per cent) and in Martinair (29.8 per cent), which are charter operators. It is a way of participating in the charter business and having some share of the profits; it also tends to keep foreign airlines away from a share in these Dutch companies, which might in theory be turned into regular carriers. Furthermore, it enables KLM to lease planes from Transavia and Martinair, and it receives fees from them for maintenance services.

In company with British Airways, KLM has a 20 per cent stake in Sabena of Belgium. Now this would appear from KLM's standpoint not to be a simple matter of revenue. While KLM–Schipol is ideal as an intercontinental hub, it cannot at the same time serve as an intra-European one. But Sabena–Brussels can be developed in this direction, to the advantage of both parties. But perhaps the most spectacular development has been KLM's acquisition of a 10 per cent stake in the US Northwest Airlines. This made history as the first international leveraged buy-out. It has led to co-operation in freight and maintenance, as well as in quality and service training. In the longer term it may lead to some route-sharing and access to more US destinations. The participation has given KLM a seat on Northwest's board.

There is a more general point to be made here, going beyond the particular strategies and alliances. It is that KLM has always been a ready partner of other airlines, has always pressed for liberalization, and has always expected to benefit from industry growth.

Computers and Codes

The various computer reservation systems (CRSs) for booking journeys by air are not only indispensable to the industry, they have become a competitive weapon. KLM is a partner in COVIA, one of the leading systems; has bought into AMADEUS, another of them; and is part owner of the Galileo Company, charged with the development and exploitation of automatic distribution systems.

There are also things airlines need to do to make their CRS attractive to travel agents. They build in extras such as hotel and car reservations, provide free terminals for agents, keep the fee that the agent pays when making a booking on your system low, and give bonuses to agents for a high number of bookings on your system.

Code-sharing is a refinement. Airlines have codes in the sense that all Pan American flights are called PA, all Lufthansa flights LH, and so on. Now when a potential customer goes to a travel agent to enquire about a flight the codes have a part to play. Suppose our passengers wants to fly from Chicago to Mulhouse, the travel agent will action the CRS and get up on the screen:

1. direct flight possibilities (if there are any);
2. double flight possibilities with the same airline, in this case, say, KLM Chicago–Schipol then KLM Schipol–Mulhouse;
3. double flight possibilities with two different airlines, say Chicago–Schipol with KLM, then Schipol–Mulhouse with Air France.

(1) and (2) above will come up on the first page, and most buying decisions are taken on the basis of the CRS first page. But if an airline agrees with another carrier to code-share, to have their flight potentially integrated with yours under your code, this transforms a (3) into a (2) as above, or moves the information from the second page to the first page, thereby increasing the likelihood of a booking. Code-sharing was an American initiative after deregulation, but the possibilities have not been lost on KLM.

The position of KLM has been discussed in some detail, not just because air transport is such a fascinating industry, but because KLM has been such an interesting player in it. It has had a concept of core business, passengers and freight, but has done a variety of things in support of this core business. These have ranged from quality programmes to cross-border acquisitions, from being an early adopter of new aircraft to being an early trainer of cabin staff, from combi aircraft to code-sharing. Few of the many things reported in this chapter are unique to KLM, yet throughout the story there is this ability to adapt and succeed in a complex industry.

The head of another airline, Jan Carlson of SAS, has canvassed the idea of the 1000 per cent factor, which has been immortalized in the Tom Peters 'Passion for Excellence' video. The idea is that companies should make their mark by doing a thousand things 1 per cent better.

This is quite a Dutch idea, even if it does come from a Swede. And it is one that fits KLM, which has wanted to compete in every dimension—cost and quality, reliability and network, technical and human. There is nothing flashy about Dutch management, but it can cope with complexity, and advance on a number of fronts at the same time. KLM is interesting as a success story, but also because it highlights this Dutch strength.

Bibliography

ACKERMAN, H. A. (1988). 'Selective Retrenchment and Growth in the Netherlands', *International Journal of Institutional Management in Higher Education*, 12/1, 1–48.

BAGLEY, CHRISTOPHER (1973). *The Dutch Plural Society*, London: Oxford University Press.

BARNETT, CORRELLI (1972). *The Collapse of British Power*, New York: William Morrow.

BARSOUX, J.-L., and LAWRENCE, P. A. (1990). *Management in France*, London: Cassell.

BOSMAN, H. W. J. (1983). *Het Nederlandse Bankwezen*, Deventer: Kluwer.

BUTTON, KENNETH (1989). 'The Deregulation of US Interstate Aviation: An assessment of Causes and Consequences (Part 1)', *Transport Review*, 9/2, 99–118.

BUTTON, KENNETH and SWANN, DENNIS (1989). 'European Community Airlines: Deregulation and Its Problems', *Journal of Common Market Studies*, 27/4, 259–82.

BUYS, ANTON (1985) 'Het "Karige" Salaris van de Nederlandse Directeur', *Management Totaal*, June–July 1985, no. 6/7.

CARLZON, JAN (1989). *Moments of Truth*, New York: Harper & Row.

CROZIER, M. (1964). *The Bureaucratic Phenomenon*, London: Tavistock.

DALTON, M. (1959). *Men Who Manage*, New York: John Wiley.

EDWARDES, MICHAEL (1983). *Back from the Brink*, London: Collins.

ELFRING, T. (1989). 'The Main Features and Underlying Causes of the Shift to Services', *Service Industries Journal*, 9/3, 337–56.

GEDDES, ANDREW (1990). 'The Netherlands: A Paradigm of Post-Industrial Society?' Ph.D. thesis, Loughborough University of Technology.

GIES, MIEP, and GOLD, ALISON LESLIE (1988). *Anne Frank Remembered*, London: Corgi Books.

GLOVER, I. A. (1978). 'Executive Career Patterns: Britain, France, Germany and Sweden', in M. F. Fores and I. A. Glover (eds.), *Manufacturing and Management*, London: HMSO.

GRIFFITHS, RICHARD T. (1980). *The Economy and Politics of the Netherlands since 1943*, The Hague: Martinus Nijhoff.

HEERDING, A. (1980). *The History of N. V. Philips Gloeilampenfabrieken*, vol. i: *The Origins of the Dutch Incandescent Lamp Industry*, Eindhoven, N. V. Philips Gloeilampenfabrieken, The Hague: Martinus Nijhoff. (English trans. Derek S. Jorden, 1985.)

HEERKENS, HANS (1990). 'Doet U er mij maar hondervijftig, staat Fokker in 2000 noch op (twee) eigenbenen', in Phijs Postmar (ed.), *Jaarboek van de Luchvaart*, Alkmaar: de Alk.

HESKETT, JOHN (1989). *Philips: A Study of the Corporate Management of Design*, London: Trefoil Publications.

HEZEWIJK, JOS VAN (1988). *De Netwerken van de Top-Elite*, Amsterdam: Uitgeverij Balans.

HOFSTEDE, G. (1975). 'The Importance of Being Dutch: National and Occupational Differences in Work-Goal Importance', *International Studies of Management and Organisation*, 5/4, 5–28.

—— (1978). *De Toekomst van ons Werk*, Leiden: Stenfert-Kroese BV.

—— (1980). *Culture's Consequences: International Differences in Work Related Values*, Beverly Hills, Calif.: Sage.

—— (1987). 'Dutch Culture's Consequences: Health, Law and Economy', Inaugural lecture, University of Limburg.

HOPKINS, ADAM (1989). *Holland*, London: Faber & Faber.

HUGGETT, FRANK E. (1983). *The Dutch Today*, The Hague: Government Publishing Office (3rd revised edn.)

HUIZINGA, J. H. (1968). *Dutch Civilization in the 17th Century*, London: Fontana.

HUTTON, S. P., and LAWRENCE, P. A. (1979). 'The Work of Production Managers: Case Studies at Manufacturing Companies in West Germany', Report to the Department of Industry, London.

—— —— (1981). *German Engineers: The Anatomy of the Profession*, London: Oxford University Press.

—— —— (1982). 'The Work of Production Managers: Case Studies of Manufacturing Companies in the United Kingdom', Report to the Science Research Council, Swindon, and the Department of Industry, London.

IDDEKINGE, P. R. A. VAN, CONSTANT, JAC G., and ALTES, A. KORFHALS (1985). *Nederland 1940–1945*, Antwerp: Zomer & Keuning Ede.

INGLEHART, R. (1977). *The Silent Revolution: Changing Values and Political Styles Among Western Publics*, Princeton, NJ: Princeton University Press.

JANSSEN, H. (1982). 'Employee Participation in Corporate Management', Rapport Neerlandais au IXe Congres International de Droit Compare.

JOHNSON, GERRY, and SCOLES, KEVAN (1989). *Exploring Corporate Strategy*, Hemel Hempstead: Prentice Hall International.

KLM (1989). *De KLM en Nederland*, Amstelveen: KLM.

KOUSBROEK, RUDY (1987). *Nederland: een bewoond gordijn*, Amsterdam: CPNB.

LAWRENCE, PETER (1980). *Managers and Management in West Germany*, London: Croom Helm.

—— (1982). 'Swedish Management: Context and Character', Report to the Social Science Research Council, London.

—— (1983). 'Operations Management: Research and Priorities', Report to the Social Science Research Council, London.

—— (1984). *Management in Action*, London: Routledge & Kegan Paul.

—— (1986). 'Management in the Netherlands: A Study in Internationalism?', Report to the Management Department, Technische Hogeschool Twente.

—— (1990). *Management in the Land of Israel*, Cheltenham: Stanley Thornes.

—— LEE, R. A. (1984). *Insight into Management*, London: Oxford University Press.

—— SPYBEY, TONY (1986). *Management and Society in Sweden*, London: Routledge & Kegan Paul.

LEEUW, RENÉ DE (1989). *Albert Plesman: Luchtvaartspionier en Visionair*, 's-Gravenhage: Uitgeverij van de Vereiniging van Nederlandse Gementen.

LOCKYER, K., and JONES, S. (1980). 'The Function Factor', *New Society* (Sept.).

MACCOBY, MICHAEL (1978). *The Gamesman*, New York: Bantam Books.

Ministry of Education and Science, Netherlands (1979). *The Institutions of Technology in the Netherlands*, The Hague.

MOKYR, JOEL (1976). *Industrialization in the Low Countries, 1795–1976*, New Haven, Conn.: Yale University Press.

Moret Group (1982). *Works Council Act*, Rotterdam: Moret Group.

MULDER, HENK (1989). *De 49 beste bedrijven om voor te werken in Nederland*, Utrecht: Veen. (Quoted excerpts translated by Peter Lawrence.)

NCD–Hay, (1985). *De Honorering van Direkteuren en Commissarissen in Nederland*, Amsterdam: Nederlandse Centrum voor Direkteuren (April).

PETERS, T. and AUSTIN, N. (1985). *A Passion for Excellence*, London: Collins.

PETERSEN, M. W. (1981). 'Financial Planning for the 1980s: A Response to Reality and Competition', *Planning for Higher Education*, 9/4, 1–5.

PHILLIPS, DEREK (1985). *De Naakte Nederlander: Kritische overpeinzingen*, Amsterdam: Uitgeverigj Bert Bakker.

PIET, SUSANNE (1987). *De Cultuur van de ondernemer*, 's-Gravenhage: BZZToH.

PUNCH, MAURICE (1976). 'Don's diary', *Times Higher Education Supplement* (25 April).

SAMPSON, ANTHONY (1985). *Empires of the Sky*, London: Coronet.

SCHAMA, SIMON (1987). *The Embarrassment of Riches*, London: Collins.

SHETTER, WILLIAM Z. (1987). *The Netherlands in Perspective*, Leiden: Martinus Nijhoff.

Social and Cultural Planning Office, The Netherlands (1982). *Social and Cultural Report 1982*, Rijswijk.

SOET, J. F. A. DE (1989). 'Today's Global Challenges, Tomorrow's Global Mission', Tenth Albert Plesman Memorial Lecture, Delft University of Technology (19 Nov.).

SYLVESTRE, J. J. (1971). 'Industrial Wage Differentials: A Two-Way Comparison', *International Labour Review*, 110/6.

TAYLOR, A. J. P. (1955). *Bismarck: The Man and the Statesman*, London: Hamish Hamilton.

TURNBULL, P., and CUNNINGHAM, M. (1981). *International Marketing and Purchasing*, London: Macmillan.

VRIES, JOHAN DE (1978). *The Netherlands Economy in the Twentieth Century*, Assen: Van Gorcum.

WARMBRUNN, WERNER (1968). *The Dutch under German Occupation 1940–45*, Stanford, Calif.: Stanford University Press.

WENLOCK, HEATHER (1990). 'The Management of Transfer of Undertakings: A Comparison of Employee Participation Practices in the United Kingdom and the Netherlands', D.Phil. thesis, St Edmund Hall, Oxford.

Wetenschappelijke Raad voor het Regeringsbeleid (1987). *Scope for Growth: Threats to and Opportunities for the Dutch Economy over the next ten years*, summary of the twenty-ninth report to the government, The Hague.

—— (1987). *Culture and Diplomacy*, The Hague.

WIENER, MARTIN (1981). *English Culture and the Decline of the Industrial Spirit 1850–1980*, Cambridge: Cambridge University Press.

WIJK, L. M. VAN (1989). 'Positioning European Airlines for Global Competition', Fourth Annual Conference on European Aviation, Amsterdam, 26–7 June.

ZAHN, ERNEST (1984). *Das Unbekannte Holland: Regenten, Rebellen und Reformatoren*, Berlin: Stedler Verlag.

ZEE, HENRI A. VAN DER (1982). *The Hunger-Winter: Occupied Holland 1944–45*, London: Jill Norman & Hobhouse.

Index